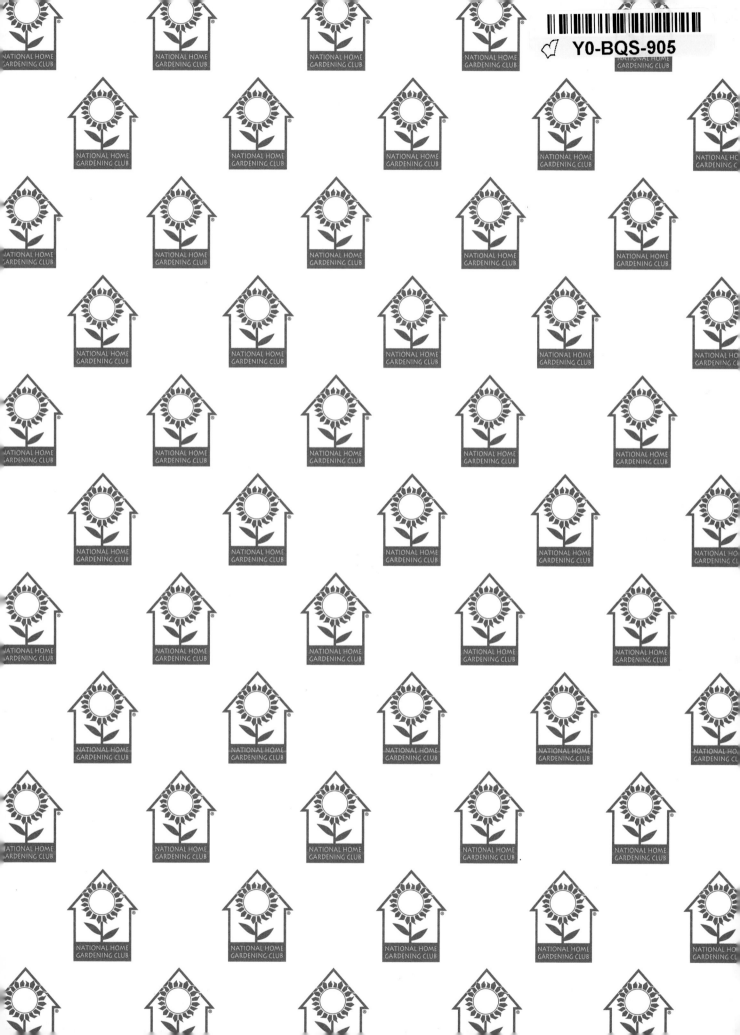

Yard & Garden Structures

Bill Hylton

Complete Gardener's Library™

YARD & GARDEN STRUCTURES

By Bill Hylton

CREDITS

Mike Vail
Vice President, New Product & Business Development

Tom Carpenter
Director of Books & New Media Development

Mark Johanson
Book Products Development Manager

Dan Cary
Photo Production Coordinator

Chris Marshall
Editorial Coordinator

Steve Anderson
Senior Book Production Assistant

Bill Hylton
Author & project designer

Bill Nelson
Series Design, Art Direction and Production

Mark Macemon
Lead Photographer

Ralph Karlen
Photography

Apple River Studios
Contributing Photographer

Craig Claeys, Bill Nelson
Illustrators

John Drigot
Technical Illustrator

Jon Hegge, John Nadeau
Senior Book Production Assistant

Brad Classen, Kari Schwab
Production Assistance

Dan Kennedy
Book Production Manager

PHOTO CREDITS
Pages 104, 111, 112
GardenStyles

CONTRIBUTING MANUFACTURER
GardenStyles
Bloomington, Minnesota
1-800-356-8890

ISBN 1-58159-046-6

National Home Gardening Club
12301 Whitewater Drive
Minnetonka, Minnesota 55343

CONTENTS

INTRODUCTION

For most of us, yards and gardens are extensions of our homes into the outdoors. They expand available living space, providing refreshing places to putter, relax and entertain. But to function well as parts of the home, your yard and garden may need some structural improvement. Maybe what's lacking is more shade or a private place to put a comfy chair. It could be that your garden is missing a crowning touch, like an arched gateway or a landscape bridge to showcase your flowers and other ornamental plants. Or it could be that your needs are entirely practical-a way to extend the growing season of your spinach or a place to store all your gardening and landscaping tools, including that lawn tractor and garden tiller.

Whatever the case, you'll find a wide range of solutions featured in the pages of this new Complete Gardner's Library volume, *Yard & Garden Structures,* published exclusively for Club members. The heart of the book is a collection of nine yard and garden projects you can build, covering a range of uses and levels of construction complexity. You'll find everything from a screened-in gazebo that will challenge your building skills to a simple compost bin you can assemble in just a few hours. Other projects include an arbor/trellis that creates an airy room in the out-of-doors, a handsome gateway to frame the entryway to a garden, and an attractive footbridge to span a waterway, pond or planting bed. We've also included no-nonsense plans for a stick-built tool shed and cold frame.

Two projects-a tractor shed and greenhouse-are built from kits. Kits can be a sensible alternative to building from scratch for many reasons. Time is a precious commodity these days. A kit saves you time at the lumberyard or home center, because you don't need to create elaborate shopping lists first, pick through stacks of lumber or drive back and forth to buy more supplies when you unexpectedly run low. Kits come with nearly everything required for installation, and it doesn't take a shop-full of tools to get highly pleasing results. You may be surprised by how easy it is to build a structure that seemed just a little beyond your skills, your available time and even your project budget.

Though some of the projects in this book may seem ambitious at first glance, don't be daunted. Each yard and garden structure is presented in methodical detail, complete with dimensioned drawings, scores of full-color photos and illustrations, or both, as well as thorough step-by-step instructions. Most projects also include an exhaustive cutting list to make your calculations easy. From layout to setting posts and from framing to installing ornamental trim, every major construction phase is clearly explained.

In the end, regardless of whether you erect an arbor from scratch or a shed from a prefabricated kit, you'll have the satisfaction of building it yourself, with sensible information guiding you every step of the way. But more importantly, you'll finish the "remodeling" your outdoor "living room" has needed all along.

IMPORTANT NOTICE

For your safety, caution and good judgment should be used when following instructions described in this book. Take into consideration your level of skill and the safety precautions related to the tools and materials shown. Neither the publisher, North American Outdoor Group, nor any of its affiliates can assume responsibility for any damage to property or persons as a result of the misuse of the information provided. Consult your local building department for information on permits, codes, regulations and laws that may apply to your project.

A few tools, a stack of lumber and some hard work are the basic ingredients for making any outdoor structure. But along with these critical elements, you'll need a solid recipe—a well-conceived plan that combines the ingredients, safely and efficiently.

OUTDOOR BUILDING BASICS

Once you've selected that per-fect shed, footbridge or gazebo project for your yard, it's important to organize your efforts systematically so the process of building your project will go smoothly and successfully. The pages that follow cover the kinds of issues you'll need to address as you proceed. In brief, here is an overview of some key points to keep in mind.

Select a site

Regardless of which type of yard or garden structure you're plan-ning, do not underestimate the importance of selecting the best site for the project. Likely as not, the structure you'll erect will become a long-term fixture on your property. Choose a spot that will maximize the utility of your project and beautify your surround-ings. For instance, if you plan to build an unscreened gazebo, steer clear of shady, damp areas that attract pests like mosquitoes. If you are building an arbor/trellis, track the sunlight at different times and anticipate how your new arbor will eventually shade the area around it. Be sure that nearby plants can tolerate partial or full shade, and plan accordingly. Even though a tool shed may be most convenient if it is positioned near the edge of your property, your next-door neighbor will probably have a view of that shed on a daily basis, too. It's always a good idea to share your plans with the neighbors before you build, so there will be no surprises or ill feelings after-ward.

Apply for a permit

Assume that any permanent structure you build will be subject to local building codes and will require a building permit. It always pays to check with your local building department and apply for the proper permit or permits whenever you build. The permit cost generally is affordable, and you'll benefit from your local building inspector's expertise when it comes to constructing a project that meets standards for public safety and solid construction. If you decide to forego the permit and the inspector pays you a visit, you may be subject to fines and even have to remove or disassemble all or part of your project so the inspector can review your work in stages. Consider a permit to be as much a part of the building process as choosing a design, buying materials or driving that first nail.

Gather your tools

You won't need a workshop full of tools to build most of the projects in this book, but a selection of the right tools will make your work easier and probably help you produce better results. See pages 10 to 11 for a review of the essential tools to consider renting, borrowing or buying, so you'll have them on hand right from the start.

Shop for building materials wisely

It's important to set a project budget up front and to stick to it as your project develops. But don't let the initial sticker shock kill your inspiration. Almost every building material you'll need to buy will be sold in a number of options and ranges of cost. Shop wisely. If your trellis project budget is tight, estimate what you might save by building with pressure-treated lumber instead of cedar or redwood. The cost savings might surprise you.

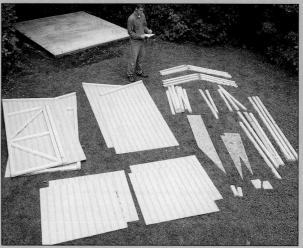

Consider kits

Prefabricated kits, like the shed kit above, are a quick, convenient and relatively inexpensive alternative to building outdoor structures from scratch. Typically, a kit will contain the framing, sheathing, roof members, fasteners and other hardware you'll need for erecting the project, along with detailed instructions. The parts come precut and ready for assembly. Normally not included in the kit are shingles, flooring and finishing materials. However, some kits do offer flooring kits sold separately. Sheds, greenhouses, gazebos, arbors and playhouses are just a few of the outdoor projects you can kit-build. Be aware that the style and size of kit-built projects may be limited, and the overall cost of the kit may exceed what you'd spend building from scratch.

Siting a project: Move from rough ideas to specific layout

In many cases, you will have a number of possibilities for siting your new structure in your yard. To determine which spot will work best, start by asking some general questions, such as how its location will impact your other yard features, like flower beds and walkways, as well as sunny and shady areas and your general sight lines. Use extension cords, rope or a garden hose to "rough out" the shape of your project and to help get a

sense for how its overall proportions will integrate with the rest of the yard. Once you've selected a site, develop an accurate layout. Using stakes or batterboards, outline the site and identify key points where digging needs to occur. Keep in mind that you still may need to move your building site if you discover too many surprises, like rocks and roots, when digging.

Before you start digging, contact your local utility companies to flag buried power lines or gas and plumbing pipes. These companies usually will stake out rights-of-way for you at no charge to avoid the possibility of having you cut a cable or pipe. And don't forget about your own utilities. Make sure you won't be interfering with your own well, septic tank or underground sprinkler system.

OUTDOOR BUILDING GUIDELINES

❑ **Watch out for buried lines.** Contact your local public utilities to identify the location of buried power lines and gas lines before you dig. Utilities will usually provide line location identification as a free service.

❑ **Research building codes.** Most municipalities enforce outdoor building restrictions. Footing and framing requirements on outdoor structures as well as minimum distance from city land and other property lines are common areas subject to regulation.

❑ **Discuss plans with your neighbors.** Your outdoor building project will likely be within the field of vision of your neighbors. As a courtesy, share plans with neighbors and give them the chance to raise objections or concerns before you start working.

❑ **Be aware of your physical limits.** Working outdoors can be highly strenuous, especially on hot, humid days. Drink plenty of water and take breaks when you can. Work with a partner, if possible.

Key information for permit applications:

• Plot location and complete address where the project will be built

• A site drawing that identifies the location of your project in relation to other permanent structures and property lines

• Detailed elevation and plan drawings that indicate overall size, materials and types of fasteners to be used

• Your estimated building cost

• Anticipated completion date

PERMITS

Whether or not you need a building permit to erect permanent outdoor structures depends on the type and size of the project and your local codes. In some places, the exterior structures presented in this book may be well outside the purview of the local building inspector. But in others, you will need to apply for a permit and have the inspector pay a visit or two to the worksite.

How do you know if you need a permit? Ask! Even before finalizing your design, consult the municipal building and zoning department where you apply for permits. These folks will lead you through the application procedure. In most cases, you'll need to complete a form that describes your project, including overall dimensions, construction details and approximate cost. You might have to submit a sketch showing where the new construction will be located in relation to your house and property lines. The permit fee is usually based on a percentage of the project's cost.

Regulations for houses are far more complex than those that govern garden outbuildings. Your inspector's primary concerns probably will be setback requirements and sound construction practices. Setback requirements refer to the minimum distance a structure must be from your property lines.

As far as sound construction practices are concerned, your building inspector can let you know of particular code requirements that apply in your area.

Work safely

Safety is no less of an issue when you are building outdoors than it is when you are working within the confines of your basement or garage workshop. You'll need protective goggles to shield your eyes when using striking tools, driving fasteners, cutting lumber or operating power equipment. Ear protection is advisable if you'll be using a circular saw, router or gas-powered equipment for long periods of time.

When cutting, routing or sanding pressure-treated lumber, wear a dust or particle mask, and do not incinerate wood scraps when you are finished. If you finish your project with a spray-on wood preservative, paint or stain, wear a cartridge-style respirator to protect your lungs from airborne particles.

Building taller outdoor structures will likely require a ladder and possibly even scaffolding. Follow the safety ratings for load and height as specified on this equipment, and exercise extra precaution when carrying supplies or operating power tools on a ladder.

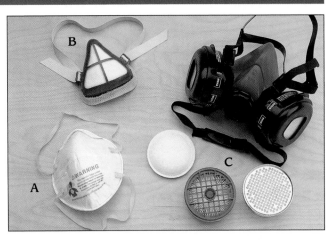

Protect against dust and fumes. A particle mask (A) or dust mask (B) are designed to keep out finer particles, like sawdust, but neither will protect you from fumes or particles from spray-on finishes. In these instances, choose a respirator (C) with the appropriate filter or cartridge instead.

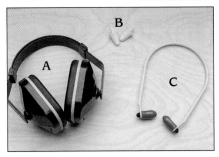

Protect your hearing when operating gas-powered machinery or most power tools. Earmuffs (A), expanding ear plugs (B) or corded ear inserts (C) all are good choices, but be sure they have a noise reduction rating (NRR) of at least 25 decibels for best hearing protection.

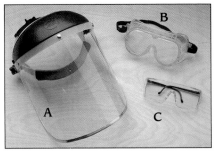

Shield your eyes from dust, wood chips and other flying debris by wearing a face shield (A), safety goggles (B) or safety glasses (C). Do not assume that your prescription glasses offer enough protection—most do not—and they won't shield your eyes from the sides.

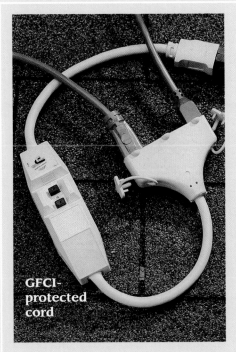

GFCI-protected cord

WORKING WITH POWER

When using power tools outdoors, avoid working in damp conditions. Also, make sure tools are plugged into a GFCI-protected outlet. GFCIs (ground-fault circuit interrupters) instantaneously cut off power if the tool or power cord short-circuits. Plug-in types are available for unprotected outlets. Or, you can buy a GFCI-protected extension cord like the one shown to the left. Also, make sure the electrical circuit has enough ampacity to handle the power tools and equipment you'll be using. A 20-amp, 110-volt circuit will handle most portable and stationary power tools. Don't overload circuits by running too many tools at once.

Ladder ratings are printed on labels that are required by law on any new ladder you purchase. Make sure your ladder is designed to support enough load and to be used in exterior conditions. Choose a Type I or Type II class extension ladder. These ratings indicate the safe weight a ladder will bear: 250 lb. for a Type I ladder; 225 lb. for Type II; and 200 lb. for a Type III. The same strength ratings are applied to stepladders.

Part of what makes building an outdoor structure enjoyable is that you don't need a shop full of high-precision woodworking tools to tackle the job. However, adding a few more tools to your arsenal and renting a few others will speed your building process, improve your accuracy and almost invariably save you time and labor in the long run. And these days, more and more power tools are cordless, which really helps when you are building outdoors and at a distance from the nearest power source. Here is an overview of the tools you may want to buy, borrow or rent when building your project.

Power tools for outdoor building will dramatically speed the process of cutting and fastening parts, and the assortment shown here is easy to transport to your jobsite. A few you'll want to consider using are: (A) power miter saw; (B) portable table saw; (C) circular saw (preferably a worm-drive saw); (D) cordless drill/driver with replaceable battery pack; (E) ½-in. corded drill; (F) reciprocating saw.

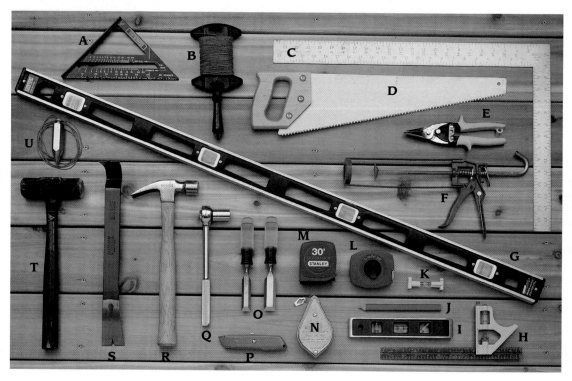

A basic set of hand tools for building outdoor structures includes: (A) speed square; (B) mason's string; (C) framing square; (D) hand saw; (E) aviator snips; (F) caulk gun; (G) carpenter's level (4 ft.); (H) combination square; (I) spirit level; (J) pencil; (K) line level; (L) 50 ft. roll tape; (M) rigid tape measure; (N) chalkline; (O) wood chisels; (P) utility knife; (Q) socket wrench; (R) hammer; (S) flat pry bar; (T) hand maul; (U) plumb bob.

A sod kicker is a hand-operated blade attached to a roller that enables you to remove sod in usable strips that can be replanted elsewhere. It shears away an even top layer of turf. Unless you are planning to remove sod often, rent this tool rather than buy it.

Sod kicker

A plate vibrator compacts subbase material more quickly and easily than a hand tamper, and it's relatively inexpensive to rent. When pouring a concrete slab, you'll want to use a plate vibrator first to ensure that the sub-base beneath the concrete is compacted uniformly.

Plate vibrator (power tamper)

PNEUMATIC NAIL GUNS

Pneumatic nail guns, powered by compressed air, offer several advantages over driving screws or hammering nails. A squeeze of the trigger both drives and countersinks the nail, and you usually can keep one hand free to hold your work. A variety of nail options are available for these tools so you can drive everything from brads to heavy framing nails. You'll need an air compressor to power most guns, but cartridge-style nailers are also available and require no compressor. Pneumatic nailers and compressors are expensive to buy but widely available to rent.

TOOL OPTIONS FOR DIGGING POST HOLES & FOOTINGS

"Clamshell"-type posthole digger

One-man gas-powered auger

Two-man gas-powered auger

If you have only a few shallow footings or post holes to dig, use a clamshell-type posthole digger (left). For deeper or larger holes, or if you have a lot of holes to dig, rent a gas-powered auger (right and inset) from a tool rental shop. Gas-powered augers come in one- and two-person models and will save you considerable time and labor over hand digging. Depending on the model, the weight of the motor either helps to drive the auger into the ground or makes withdrawing the auger easier.

Lumber for outdoor building projects

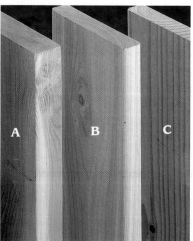

Parts of your outdoor structure that are sheltered from the elements or painted can be made of ordinary dimensional softwood (A). Use cedar (B) or pressure-treated lumber (C) for parts like posts and railings that come in contact with the ground or must remain exposed. Cypress and redwood are other options, depending on your region.

Options for creating footings

Masonry-related materials for footings include: (A) concrete tube forms (8- and 12-in.-dia. shown); (B) premixed concrete; (C) precast concrete piers (an alternative to pouring footings).

BUYING LUMBER & FASTENERS

Lumber, fasteners and miscellenous metal hardware will make up the bulk of your project expense. Study your lumber and fastener options so you can maximize your project budget dollars.

Lumber: When you go to buy lumber, make up a shopping list with columns that identify the sizes, lengths and quantity you need. For each lumber item, add 5% to 10% extra to allow for waste, lumber defects and building errors. If possible, hand-pick your lumber at the yard, even if you plan to have it delivered, to get the best boards in the stack.

Creating a shopping list for your project can be time-consuming, but it will save countless trips to the lumberyard. Making a shopping list is not simply a matter of adding up the total length of all your project parts and dividing by common board lengths to determine the amount you'll need. Instead, you must consider how your project parts will fit on the board lengths you buy and how you can make most efficent use of the lumber. It helps to draw various board sizes to smaller scale and sketch your parts right on the boards. Use these sketches as cutting diagrams later.

Fasteners & hardware: Outdoor structures should be built with corrosion-resistant fasteners. The most common and least expensive option is to buy galvanized steel fasteners. However, galvanized coatings will react with the tannins in some woods, like cedar, creating small black spots. The stains are harmless, but they can be unsightly. Other fastener options that won't stain your wood include teflon-coated, aluminum, stainless-steel and brass, but these will be more expensive and are not made in all styles.

A host of galvanized metal brackets is available for connecting posts, beams and joists. While this hardware is sturdy and convenient, it isn't particularly attractive for connections that show. For aesthetic reasons, we opted to use other fastening methods, like toe-nailing, for most of the projects in this book.

Shopping for building supplies to construct an outdoor structure can be a bit daunting, especially if you've never built a sizable project before. You'll likely need framing lumber, plywood sheathing, a variety of screws, nails, bolts and nuts and an assortment of galvanized metal hanger hardware. If your structure has a roof, you'll need shingles and building paper, roofing nails, roofing cement and metal drip edge. Depending on the condition of the construction site, you may need to buy a load of sub-base material (usually compactible gravel) along with suitable posts and piers or tube forms and concrete.

To make the shopping task less intimidating and a little more affordable, here are a few tips to keep in mind:

• Think of your project as a series of smaller projects that start from the ground up. Make a separate shopping list for your project's base, framing and sheathing, windows or doors, decking and railings and roof. Shorter lists will give each trip to the home center or lumberyard more focus and will help you avoid estimation errors.

• If possible, buy your supplies over an extended period of time, so you can do some materials comparison shopping and take advantage of sales as they occur.

The following pages cover a variety of building materials you may need for your project.

Coarse sand is used as a base material for setting landscape pavers and natural stones as well as beneath concrete. It offers fair drainage and adequate compaction around posts and piers and beneath slabs.

Pea gravel is used mostly as a drainage material, but it can also double as a border treatment around plantings. It is not recommended for use as a base material beneath pavers or concrete slabs.

Compactible gravel is an inexpensive subbase material used widely for landscape construction projects. Known in some regions as "Class V" or "Class II" (lower numbers denote smaller aggregate), it improves drainage and can be tamped to create a stable base.

River rock is used mostly as a drainage material when backfilling or providing drainage in a post hole. It can also be used for decorative or loose-fill purposes. River rock is sold according to the diameter of the stones (3/8 in., 3/4 in., and 1 1/2 in. are typical). As a general rule, use smaller diameter stones for drainage fill. 1 1/2-in.-dia. river rock is shown here.

Loose-fill choices

If you want to create ground cover around plant bedding areas or simple walkways through your yard and to garden projects, a number of natural loose-fill options are available. Smaller aggregates, mulch and bark are the most common. These materials are commonly sold by the bag or by the yard, depending upon where you shop and how much you need. Examples shown here are: (A) crushed limestone; (B) 3/8- to 3/4-in.-dia. river rock; (C) cypress mulch and; (D) cedar bark chips.

Concrete footings (See pages 27 to 30) extend down into the ground and create a stable base for posts and joists. A footing can be formed by either pouring concrete directly into a hole in the ground or by filling a tubular form (as shown here). Tubular forms keep the sides of the hole from collapsing and they also slow down the curing speed of the concrete, which strengthens it.

Concrete slabs (See pages 127 to 132) provide a broad, stable base and a hard, flat surface for larger structures, like sheds and gazebos. Generally, several inches of earth are removed from the slab area first and replaced with a compacted layer of gravel or sand to drain water away from the slab and keep it from shifting later. A wood form is constructed to give the slab its shape, then wet concrete is poured directly into the form.

ESTIMATING CONCRETE

Concrete is calculated and sold in volume units of cubic feet and cubic yards. You'll need to determine the total volume of concrete required for your footings or slab in order to purchase an accurate amount. If you buy ready-mix concrete that comes delivered in a truck, your supplier will want your estimate in terms of cubic yards. Should you decide to buy premixed dry concrete instead from your local home center, it comes packaged in 60-pound bags that yield ½ cubic ft. Doing the math can be a bit befuddling, especially when it comes to calculating the volume of tubular footings. Fortunately, a handy chart is printed right on the pre-mix bags to help you estimate the number of bags you need for various-sized slabs and footings. Your ready-mix supplier can help you determine yardage if you explain the dimensions of your slab or the diameter, height and number of footings you need to pour. Or, use the chart below to help you figure what you need, based on some common concrete yields. If you calculate your own quantities, round up 10% to be safe.

Concrete quantity	Yields		
	4-IN.-THICK SLAB	8-IN.-DIA. FOOTING	12-IN.-DIA. FOOTING
¼ yard (14 bags*)	20 square ft.	14 @ 16 in. deep 5 @ 42 in. deep	6 @ 16 in. deep 2 @ 42 in. deep
½ yard (27 bags)	40 square ft.	28 @ 16 in. deep 10 @ 42 in. deep	12 @ 16 in. deep 4 @ 42 in. deep
1 yard (54 bags)	80 square ft.	57 @ 16 in. deep 21 @ 42 in. deep	25 @ 16 in. deep 9 @ 42 in. deep

*Bag quantities are 60-pound dry-mixed concrete

Ready-mix. When you purchase concrete and have it delivered, the concrete comes already mixed and ready to pour. Buying ready-mix is economical when you need several yards of concrete. You'll pay a delivery charge regardless of the size of the order, which makes batches of 1 yard or less more expensive. Have helpers with wheelbarrows on hand when the concrete arrives and create a path with boards to protect your lawn and make smooth wheelbarrow runs. You'll need to move quickly.

Rent a mixing trailer when you need more concrete than can feasibly be mixed in a wheelbarrow. You can haul this mixer behind your truck or car. They come powered by either a gas or electric motor. Some trailers can be filled with ready-mix at your concrete supplier so you are ready to pour when you get home.

MIXING CONCRETE YOURSELF

Mixing concrete is hard work, and the logistics can be daunting. You have two options: If your project requires only small amounts—setting posts, for example—consider buying premixed concrete in a bag. It comes already packaged in the proper ratio of portland cement, sand and gravel. All you need to do is add water and blend the mixture in a wheelbarrow with a hoe.

A second alternative is to purchase the ingredients in bulk and mix them yourself—a cheaper but more labor-intensive process. Portland cement is sold in 1-cubic-ft. bags weighing 94 pounds. The gravel and sand are sold in bulk, by weight. If you have a pickup or a trailer, you can buy the ingredients, haul them home and shovel them into piles. Otherwise, you can have sand and gravel delivered by the truckload.

When mixing from scratch in a wheelbarrow, mix the cement and sand first. They must be blended to a uniform color, showing neither light nor dark streaks. Add water little by little, until the entire mixture is evenly moist. Mix in the gravel last. If you add gravel before the water it probably will be too difficult to mix by hand. If you get carried away with the water and the mix seems too soupy, add small amounts of cement, sand and gravel in the same proportions you used in the original mix.

For those instances where you use a power mixer, you'll blend the mixture in a different order. With the mixer stopped, load in the gravel and some water. Start the mixer, and while it is running, add the sand, cement and (as long as the mix seems to need it) more water. Keep the mixer running for at least three minutes, or until the contents are a uniform color. Add water a little at a time until you get a mix of the right consistency. Pour the concrete as soon as possible.

If you are mixing concrete yourself, here are some recommended proportions for slabs and footings.

Slabs (light traffic):
1 part cement, 2 parts sand, four parts gravel

Slabs (heavy traffic):
1 part cement, 1½ parts sand, three parts gravel

Footings:
1 part cement, 2 parts sand, four parts gravel

Treat end grain with sealer. Even if you apply no finish at all to your outdoor project, coat the ends of project parts with waterproofing wood sealer to keep them from absorbing moisture and eventually rotting. This is especially important with posts or joists that come in contact with the ground.

FINISHING PRESSURE-TREATED WOOD

Despite the infusion of chemicals into pressure-treated wood, it still will take finishes such as stains and paints with pleasing results. One thing to keep in mind when finishing treated lumber is that you should let it dry thoroughly first, before topcoating with a finish. The labels on cans of exterior finishes will usually specify a recommended drying time for treated lumber (often several months). Be sure to follow the instructions on the can carefully, just as you would for applying a finish to other exterior woods.

At some point in the building process, you'll find yourself standing in the paint department of the local home center, staring at the wide assortment of finishes available to you. The world of exterior wood finishes used to be simple. Once, there were only three basic categories: paint, stain or varnish. No more. While those broad categories are still useful, they aren't as clear-cut anymore. What, for example, distinguishes paint from solid-color stain?

To choose a finish, first ask yourself what you want the finish to accomplish. The ideal finish would never need maintenance, would keep moisture out of the wood to prevent cracking and cupping, would prevent degradation from the sun's ultraviolet (UV) rays and inhibit fungal growth. There is no such finish, of course. All finishes do provide some protection from moisture, the sun and fungi, but each type of finish is better at some of these jobs than others. And the amount and kind of maintenance required varies with the finish.

In choosing an exterior wood finish, ask yourself a few questions:

• Do I want the wood grain to show through? Or do I need to conceal it?

• How much time and effort am I willing to expend for surface preparation, like priming, before applying the finish?

• Am I willing to spend the time recoating periodically, or do I want the finish to last indefinitely?

• Do I really need to apply a finish at all, or am I willing to allow the wood to age naturally and turn gray?

See the next page for an overview of the basic finish categories available for protecting outdoor structures.

Exterior wood finish options

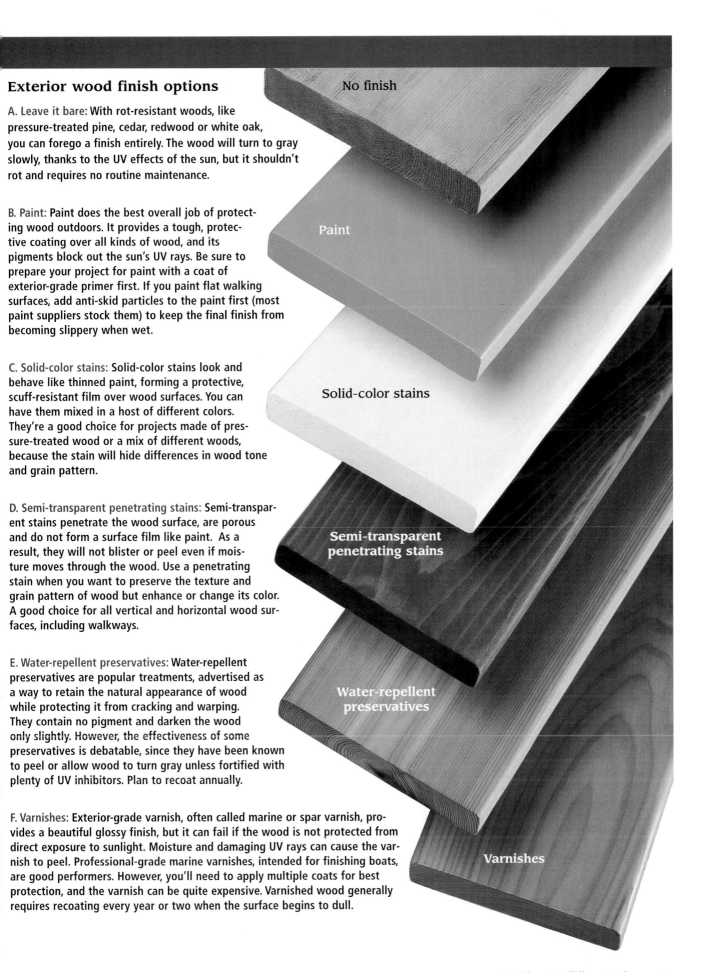

No finish

Paint

Solid-color stains

Semi-transparent
penetrating stains

Water-repellent
preservatives

Varnishes

A. Leave it bare: With rot-resistant woods, like pressure-treated pine, cedar, redwood or white oak, you can forego a finish entirely. The wood will turn to gray slowly, thanks to the UV effects of the sun, but it shouldn't rot and requires no routine maintenance.

B. Paint: Paint does the best overall job of protecting wood outdoors. It provides a tough, protective coating over all kinds of wood, and its pigments block out the sun's UV rays. Be sure to prepare your project for paint with a coat of exterior-grade primer first. If you paint flat walking surfaces, add anti-skid particles to the paint first (most paint suppliers stock them) to keep the final finish from becoming slippery when wet.

C. Solid-color stains: Solid-color stains look and behave like thinned paint, forming a protective, scuff-resistant film over wood surfaces. You can have them mixed in a host of different colors. They're a good choice for projects made of pressure-treated wood or a mix of different woods, because the stain will hide differences in wood tone and grain pattern.

D. Semi-transparent penetrating stains: Semi-transparent stains penetrate the wood surface, are porous and do not form a surface film like paint. As a result, they will not blister or peel even if moisture moves through the wood. Use a penetrating stain when you want to preserve the texture and grain pattern of wood but enhance or change its color. A good choice for all vertical and horizontal wood surfaces, including walkways.

E. Water-repellent preservatives: Water-repellent preservatives are popular treatments, advertised as a way to retain the natural appearance of wood while protecting it from cracking and warping. They contain no pigment and darken the wood only slightly. However, the effectiveness of some preservatives is debatable, since they have been known to peel or allow wood to turn gray unless fortified with plenty of UV inhibitors. Plan to recoat annually.

F. Varnishes: Exterior-grade varnish, often called marine or spar varnish, provides a beautiful glossy finish, but it can fail if the wood is not protected from direct exposure to sunlight. Moisture and damaging UV rays can cause the varnish to peel. Professional-grade marine varnishes, intended for finishing boats, are good performers. However, you'll need to apply multiple coats for best protection, and the varnish can be quite expensive. Varnished wood generally requires recoating every year or two when the surface begins to dull.

ENTERTAINMENT STRUCTURES

Few pleasures in life rival the time spent outdoors on a beautiful afternoon or evening. Whether you're relaxing with a good book, hosting a garden party or barbecue, or simply soaking up some sun, that time will be even more enjoyable if your surroundings are pleasant, attractive and well appointed. Plantings, groundcovers and the general condition of your yard go a long way toward letting your surroundings shine to their fullest potential. But a perfectly placed, well-crafted structure or two can be the key ingredient in transforming a nice yard into a showplace you're proud to call your outdoor home.

GAZEBO

A luxurious retreat that graces any setting, this gazebo offers the ultimate in sophistication. Follow along as we show you how to build one in your own yard or garden.

All sorts of gazebo designs are possible. We tend to think of them as being hexagonal or octagonal, but a gazebo can be square or rectangular, even oblong. It can stand alone or be incorporated into a deck. Style is a big part of design. We chose a style with a Victorian flavor for our gazebo. The shape of the railing balusters and the corner brackets are the primary contributors to that Victorian flavor.

The construction of this gazebo owes a lot to the prefab units that are so commonplace these days. Many of the parts can be cut in the shop, if you have one, and elements like the railing and the screen frames can be preassembled in a workshop, then hauled to the site for installation.

This gazebo project is not especially complex or time-consuming to make, as far as gazebos go. But neither is it designed with the beginning carpenter in mind. It involves some of the trickier construction techniques, including cutting compound miters, as well as production style manufacturing of some parts (especially the balusters) that would be very unwieldy without good power tools. If you are just beginning to develop your carpentry skills, consider a gazebo kit. And read this chapter closely. It is a thorough treatment of how these charming structures are made.

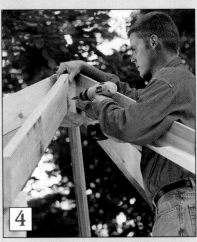

Gazebo Project:
A 7-step overview

1. Lay out the site & pour the footings (27 to 30)
2. Build the undercarriage (30 to 34)
3. Install the decking (34 to 37)
4. Install the roof supports (37 to 42)
5. Build the roof (42 to 46)
6. Install railings & trim (46 to 49)
7. Finishing touches (50 to 54)

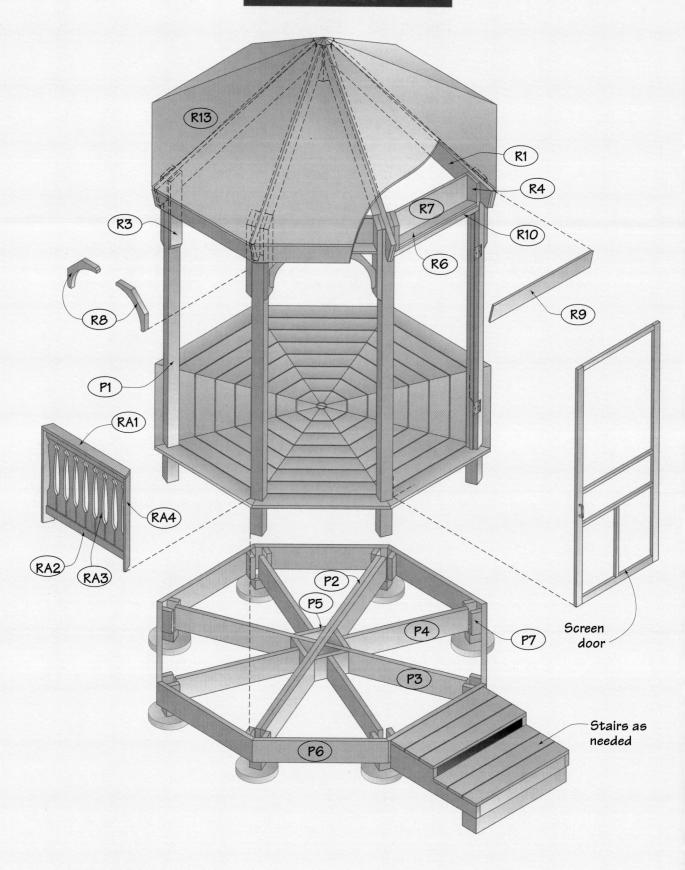

R13

R1

R4

R3

R7

R10

R6

R8

R9

P1

RA1

RA4

RA2

RA3

P2

P5

P4

P7

P3

P6

Screen door

Stairs as needed

OVERALL DIMENSIONS ($97^1/_4 \times 97^1/_4 \times 134^5/_8"$)

KEY	PART NAME	QTY.	SIZE	MATERIAL
PLATFORM				
P1	POSTS	8	$3^1/_2 \times 3^1/_2 \times 96^5/_8"$	CEDAR
P2	DOUBLED JOIST	2	$1^1/_2 \times 7^1/_4 \times 89"$	PRESSURE TREATED
P3	LONG JOIST	2	$1^1/_2 \times 7^1/_4 \times 43"$	PRESSURE TREATED
P4	SHORT JOIST	4	$1^1/_2 \times 7^1/_4 \times 37^{11}/_{16}"$	PRESSURE TREATED
P5	JOIST HUB BLOCKING	4	$1^1/_2 \times 7^1/_4 \times 10^7/_{16}"$	PRESSURE TREATED
P6	RIM JOIST	8	$1^1/_2 \times 7^1/_4 \times 38^9/_{16}"$	CEDAR
P7	RIM JOIST BLOCKING	16	$1^1/_2 \times 3^1/_2 \times 7^1/_4"$	CEDAR
P8	DECKING - RING 1	8	$1 \times 5^1/_2 \times 39^3/_{16}"$	CEDAR
P9	DECKING - RING 2	8	$1 \times 5^1/_2 \times 34^3/_8"$	CEDAR
P10	DECKING - RING 3	8	$1 \times 5^1/_2 \times 29^5/_8"$	CEDAR
P11	DECKING - RING 4	8	$1 \times 5^1/_2 \times 24^7/_8"$	CEDAR
P12	DECKING - RING 5	8	$1 \times 5^1/_2 \times 20^1/_8"$	CEDAR
P13	DECKING - RING 6	8	$1 \times 5^1/_2 \times 15^5/_{16}"$	CEDAR
P14	DECKING - RING 7	8	$1 \times 5^1/_2 \times 10^9/_{16}"$	CEDAR
P15	DECKING - RING 8	8	$1 \times 5^1/_2 \times 5^{13}/_{16}"$	CEDAR
P16	DECKING CENTER	1	$1 \times 2^9/_{16} \times 2^9/_{16}"$	CEDAR
ROOF				
R1	RAFTERS	8	$1^1/_2 \times 5^1/_2 \times 63^1/_2"$	CEDAR
R2	FILLER BLOCK	6	$1 \times 3^1/_2 \times 9^1/_2"$	CEDAR
R3	VERTICAL BATTEN	14	$1^1/_2 \times 3^1/_2 \times 24"$	CEDAR
R4	BATTEN AT DOOR	2	$1^1/_2 \times 3^1/_2 \times 5^1/_8"$	CEDAR
R5	HUB	1	$5^1/_2 \times 5^1/_2 \times 12"$	CEDAR
R6	HORIZONTAL FRIEZE	8	$3/_4 \times 3^1/_8 \times 30^3/_4"$	CEDAR
R7	VERTICAL FRIEZE	8	$3/_4 \times 8^7/_8 \times 28^{11}/_{16}"$	CEDAR
R8	BRACKET	14	$1^1/_2 \times 5^1/_2 \times 15^5/_8"$	CEDAR
R9	FASCIA	8	$3/_4 \times 5^3/_4 \times 40"$	CEDAR
R10	DOOR HEADER	1	$1^1/_2 \times 3^1/_2 \times 33^1/_2"$	CEDAR
R11	FILLER AT HEADER	2	$3/_4 \times 1^1/_4 \times 33^1/_2"$	CEDAR
R12	DOOR STOP	3	$1/_2 \times 1 \times 80"$	CEDAR
R13	SHEATHING	8	$3/_4 \times 40 \times 58"$	AC PLYWOOD
RAILING				
RA1	CAP RAIL	7	$1 \times 1/_4 \times 33^1/_2"$	CEDAR
RA2	TOP/BOTTOM RAIL	14	$1^1/_2 \times 2^1/_2 \times 31^3/_8"$	CEDAR
RA3	BALUSTER	56	$3/_4 \times 3^1/_2 \times 24"$	CEDAR
RA4	BATTEN	14	$3/_4 \times 3^1/_2 \times 31"$	CEDAR
SCREEN (QUANTITY TO MAKE 7 SCREENS)				
S1	STILE	14	$3/_4 \times 1^1/_2 \times 82^3/_4"$	CEDAR
S2	TOP RAIL	7	$3/_4 \times 1^1/_2 \times 29"$	CEDAR
S3	BOTTOM RAIL	7	$3/_4 \times 3^1/_2 \times 29"$	CEDAR
S4	HORIZONTAL MULLION	7	$3/_4 \times 1^1/_2 \times 29"$	CEDAR
S5	FILLER	7	$3/_4 \times 3/_4 \times 29"$	CEDAR
S6	MOUNTING BATTEN	8	$3/_4 \times 1^1/_4 \times 82^3/_4"$	CEDAR
HARDWARE REQUIRED				
	SCREENING	50 linear ft.	32-36" wide roll	
	SCREEN DOOR	1	$32 \times 80"$	
	HINGES	2	$2 \times 3"$	
	HANDLE	1		
	POST ANCHORS/J BOLTS	8		
	BUILDING PAPER	100 sq.ft		
	SHINGLES	100 sq.ft		YOUR CHOICE
	SCREW EYES & HOOKS	28 PAIR		
	CARRIAGE BOLTS	32	$3/_8 \times 6^1/_2"$	W/NUTS & WASHERS
	DECKING SCREWS	2"		
	NAILS			
	LAG SCREWS	8	$5/_{16} \times 4"$	W/WASHERS

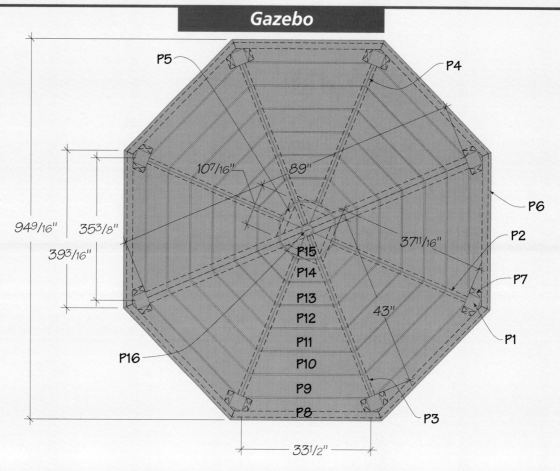

PLAN VIEW - FLOOR PLATFORM (FRAMING/DECKING)

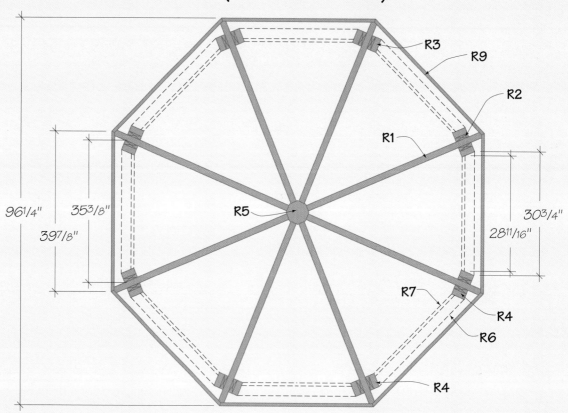

PLAN VIEW - ROOF FRAMING

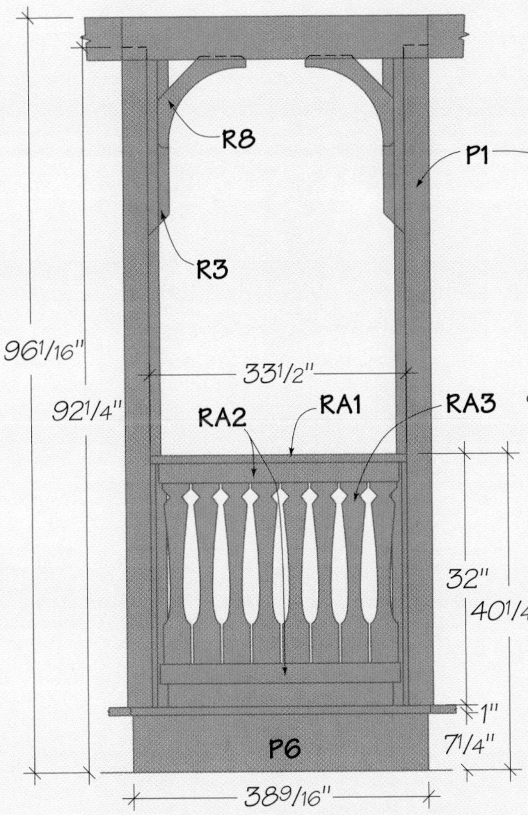

R8

R3

R9

R10

P1

S2

S1

$11/2''$

$96^{1/16}''$

$92^{1/4}''$

$33^{1/2}''$

RA2   RA1   RA3

$32''$

$40^{1/4}''$

$1''$

P6

$7^{1/4}''$

$38^{9/16}''$

ELEVATION AT TYPICAL SIDE

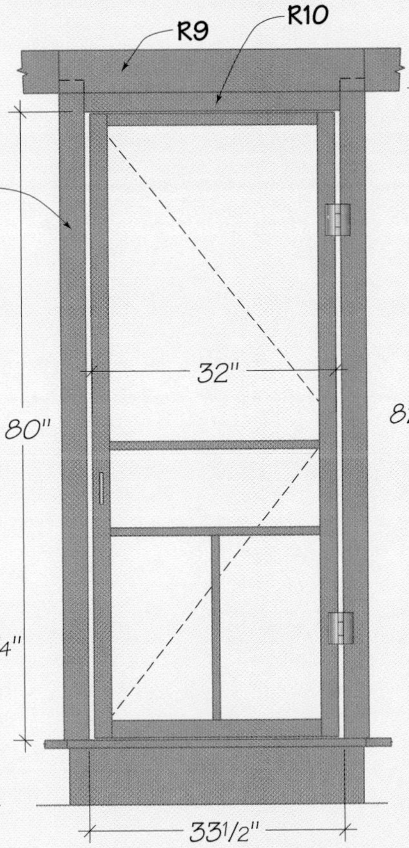

$80''$

$32''$

$33^{1/2}''$

ELEVATION AT DOOR

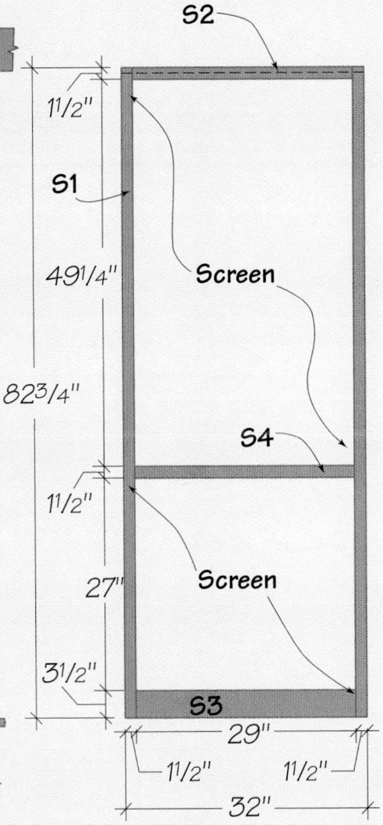

$49^{1/4}''$

Screen

$82^{3/4}''$

S4

$11/2''$

$27''$

Screen

$31/2''$

S3

$29''$

$11/2''$ $11/2''$

$32''$

SCREEN FRAME

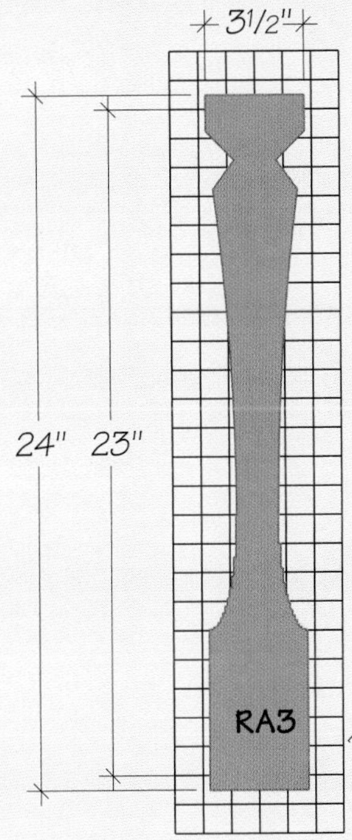

$31/2''$

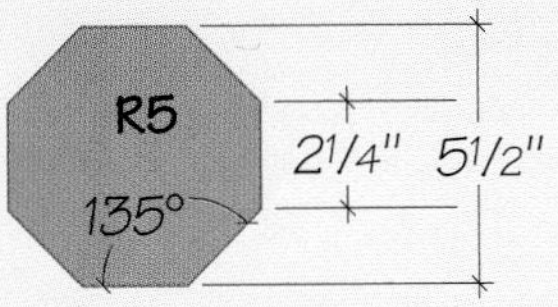

R5

$2^{1/4}''$ $5^{1/2}''$

$135°$

HUB PATTERN

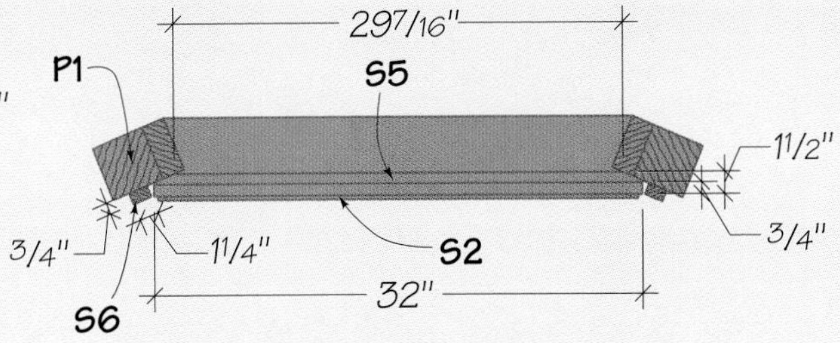

$29^{7/16}''$

P1   S5

$11/2''$

$3/4''$ $11/4''$ S2 $3/4''$

S6 $32''$

PLAN VIEW AT SCREEN

$24''$ $23''$

RA3

1" Squares

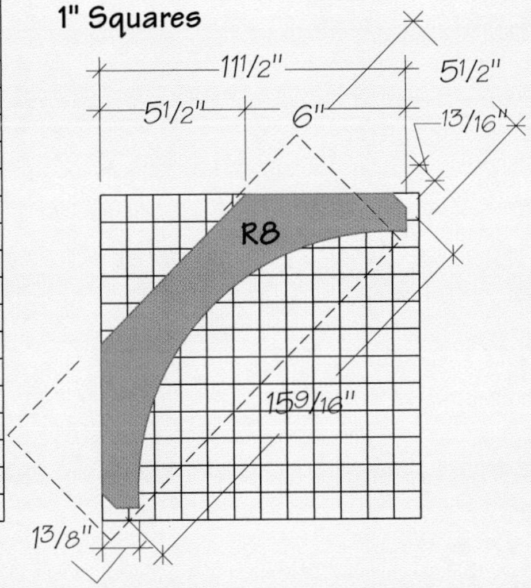

$11^{1/2}''$ $5^{1/2}''$

$5^{1/2}''$ $13/16''$

6"

R8

$15^{9/16}''$

$13/8''$

$5^{1/2}''$

$63^{1/2}''$

$53°$

R1

$73°$

BALUSTER PATTERN   **CORNER BRACKET PATTERN** 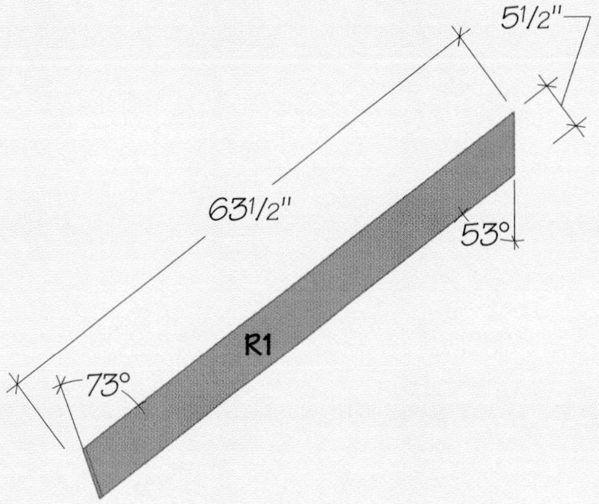   **RAFTER PATTERN**

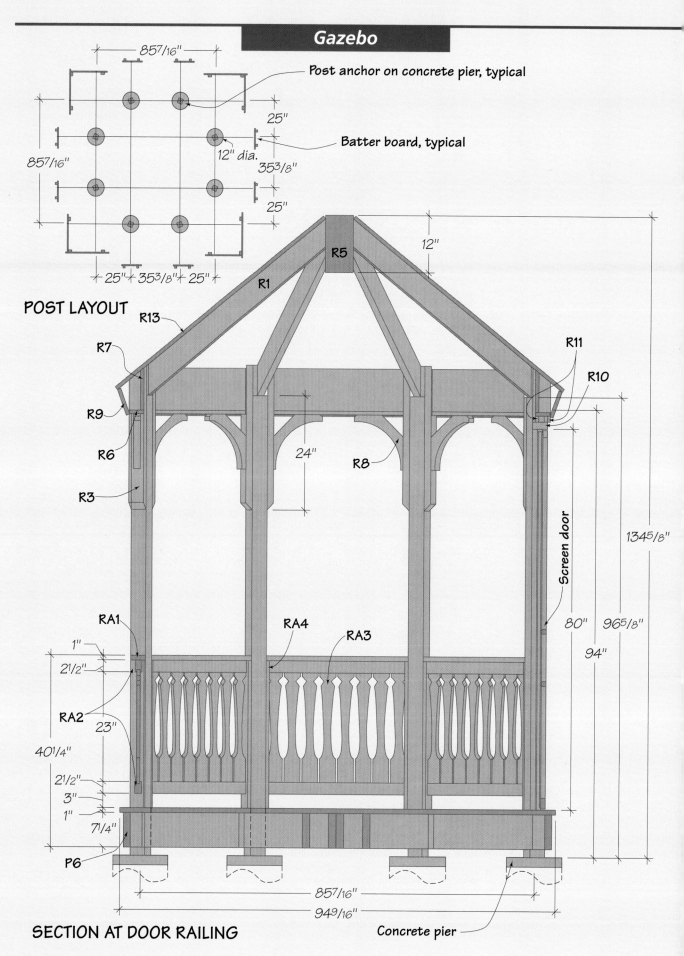

Post anchor on concrete pier, typical

85⁷/16"

25"

Batter board, typical

85⁷/16"

12" dia.

35³/8"

25"

POST LAYOUT

25" 35³/8" 25"

R5

12"

R1

R13

R7

R11

R10

R9

R6

R8

R3

24"

Screen door

134⁵/8"

RA1

1"

2¹/2"

RA4

RA3

80" 96⁵/8"

94"

RA2

23"

40¹/4"

2¹/2"

3"

1"

7¹/4"

P6

85⁷/16"

94⁹/16"

SECTION AT DOOR RAILING

Concrete pier

Building a gazebo is a major undertaking for even the most experienced home carpenter. It requires some familiarity with all the basic construction skills, from working with concrete to framing to finish carpentry. It also requires a good deal of organization and project coordination. You'll need to draw up detailed plans, get a permit and arrange to have the structure inspected at key points. But don't be discouraged. After all the hard work and attention to detail, you'll emerge with a classically beautiful outdoor structure that will dramatically improve your ability to enjoy your yard and garden. And if you can manage to build a gazebo, you'll know you can tackle just about any outdoor building project.

ONE: Lay out the the site & pour the footings

Laying out the gazebo building site is best accomplished by driving stakes into the ground and running strings from stake to stake, outlining the perimeter of the project. The strings will help you determine where to remove sod and exactly where to dig holes for post footings. The strings also help you determine when the site is level.

You need some pointed wooden stakes, a small sledge hammer (maul), mason's string, a 4 ft. carpenter's level, a line level, a framing square, and a long tape measure. It's also good to have a helper.

We used batterboards and mason's string to establish the layout for the gazebo posts. Start by setting up stakes and batterboards (the crosspieces on the assemblies) so the batterboard is positioned one or two feet behind a rough corner location. Drive another stake so it forms a perpendicular corner with the first stakes *(See Photo 1:1)*. Then, connect the new stake to the original batterboard with another batterboard (perpendicular

Crosspieces

Photo 1:1 Drive pairs of wood stakes a couple of feet directly behind the corners of the planned project site. Attach horizontal crosspieces to the stakes to form batterboards. By tying mason's strings to the crosspieces of the batterboards and adjusting the height and position of the strings and crosspieces you can pinpoint the post locations for your layout. Here, a third stake and second crosspiece are being installed to form a corner.

Photo 1:2 Even though the gazebo has 8 corners, you'll need to start with a square layout area (See *Post Layout* illustration, previous page). In the photo, the mason's strings are checked for square using the 3-4-5 triangle method: measure out from the corner 3 ft. in one direction and 4 ft. in the other; mark the points with tape; adjust the positions of the strings until the distance between the points is exactly 5 ft.

to the first) at the same height. Tie a mason's string to each batterboard and stretch them out along what you intend to be the edges of the project's footprint. When you are a foot or two beyond the adjacent corners of the project, set up another batterboard at each corner. Stretch the string tight and tie it to this new stake. Check the string with a line level and adjust the height of one of the new batterboards to bring the string to a level position (See Tip, next page). Use this string as a reference for leveling other strings. Position the bat-

terboards at the opposite corner from the corner at which you started. Tie mason's strings to the batterboards to establish the four corners of the square. As shown, the square should have 85½-in.-long sides.

Check the strings to make sure they are square to one another and the correct distance apart. This will require you to slide each string back and forth along the batterboard it is attached to until the layout is correct. Use a squaring method *(such as the 3-4-5 method shown in Photo 1:2)* to make sure

Photo 1:3 Once you have tied and adjusted all the strings to identify the post locations, use a plumb bob to transfer the locations (the points where the strings intersect) to the ground. Drive a stake to mark the position of each post.

the strings are square. Mark the position of each string on the batterboards in case they slip out of position or need to be removed temporarily.

Once the corners of the string layout are squared up, set up more batterboards (two per side, spaced evenly, as shown in the *Post Layout* diagram on page 26). Tie mason's strings between opposing, intermediate batterboards, level them and adjust them until the distances between strings match those shown on the diagram. Mark their positions on the batterboards.

Drop a plumb line from each point (eight points in total) where a cross-string is attached to one of the original squared strings *(See Photo 1:3)*. Drive a stake at each spot to mark centerpoints for digging post holes.

Double-check the layout to

Photo 1:4 The completed layout of the project area identifies exactly where to dig post holes and allows you to gauge the depth of the holes. Mark the positions of the strings on the batter boards, then remove the strings before you start digging. Re-tie the strings so you can check your work when you finish digging.

LEVELING LINES ON BATTERBOARDS

To level the mason's strings when using batterboards, suspend a line level from one layout line and adjust the batter board up or down as needed until the layout line is level. Secure the batter board to the stakes at this height. This will set the height "permanently," allowing you to adjust the line from side to side as you square up the layout. Use the height of the first line as the baseline for setting additional lines to the same height.

make sure the corners are square, the strings are the correct distance apart and all the strings are level. Make sure the marks on the batterboards reflect the correct string positions. When you are done leveling the strings and marking the batterboards *(See Photo 1:4),* you can remove all the strings tem-

DEALING WITH ROOTS & ROCKS WHEN DIGGING

Gas-powered augers will not cut through large roots or magically wind their way past rocks. If you strike a large rock while digging a post hole, you have two options: either grab a shovel and pry bar and see if you can extract or move the offending rock; or relocate the structure.

A large root can be more of a problem. It is very tempting to try to cut through roots with a power auger—it is even reasonable to expect your auger to chew through smaller to medium sized roots. But if you feel the blade begin to bog down, stop the machine immediately. In trying to work through tough obstacles, the blade can become embedded. Since many power augers don't have reverse gearing, a stuck blade presents quite a problem. It will leave you few solutions other than disengaging the motor and trying to turn the drive shaft in a reverse direction with a pipe wrench to free the blade. This is exactly as difficult and laborious as it sounds.

Before you begin digging, arm yourself with a few tools to deal with those unavoidable obstructions: a "clamshell" post hole digger for removing dirt around the obstruction; a heavy pry bar for dislodging stones; and a "spud bar" (a weighted bar with a flat cutting blade) for cutting roots. And as always, check with your utility companies before digging (See page 8).

Photo 1:5 Dig the post holes. We used a gas-powered auger since our post holes needed to be about 4 ft. deep and there were eight of them. The holes should be at least 18 in. deep and extend a few inches past the frost line for your area. Make sure you have your yard flagged for buried lines before you start digging (See page 8).

Photo 1:6 Set tubular forms (if needed) in the holes and level and plumb the forms. Pack gravel or dirt around the forms to hold them in place.

Photo 1:7 Overfill the forms slightly with concrete, then shape the concrete surface with a masonry trowel to create a slight crown that sheds water.

Photo 1:8 Before the concrete sets, transfer the locations of the post centerpoints to the footing. Set a J-bolt (for attaching post anchors) into the concrete at each centerpoint. The threaded end should stick up about 1 in.

porarily to create access for digging post holes.

Dig the post holes *(See Photo 1:5)*. A power auger is the quickest tool for creating the post holes, but in rocky or rooty soil, such a machine can be tough for even the burliest of handymen to control. The alternative is a clam-shell post hole digger. By whichever means you choose, dig the post holes, making sure each one extends down below the frost line in your area.

If the soil is firm and your post holes have straight walls, you can pour the concrete directly into the holes. In loose soil conditions, however, tubular forms may be necessary. Cut the forms to length (a reciprocating saw or hand saw works well) and place a form in each post hole (the top should be a couple of inches above grade). Pack gravel around the outside of the form to hold it plumb and centered *(See Photo 1:6)*.

NOTE: Arrange for inspection of the footing holes before pouring concrete.

Calculate the amount of concrete needed to fill the holes/forms to grade and choose a delivery method (See pages 14 to 15). Overfill the forms or post holes slightly with concrete. As you pour the concrete, work the material lightly with a stick to eliminate air bubbles. Trowel the surface to smooth it and to crown it slightly so it sheds water *(See Photo 1:7)*.

Working quickly, re-tie the mason's strings in their marked positions on the batterboards. Use the lines as references for positioning a J-bolt at the centerpoint of each post location (don't just center the bolt on the footing.) Set a J-bolt into the wet concrete at each centerpoint *(See Photo 1:8)*. Allow the concrete to set up overnight before proceeding.

Photo 2:1 Attach a metal post anchor to the J-bolt in each footing. Position the post anchors so one of the nailing flanges is square to the center of the layout. To secure the post anchors, thread a washer over the threaded top of the J-bolt, then tighten a nut onto the bolt with a socket wrench.

Nailing flanges

Photo 2:2 Screw 2 × 4 braces to two adjacent sides of each post, about halfway up. Fit a post level onto each post and use it as a guide for leveling and plumbing the post. When the post is in the correct position, drive a stake into the ground next to the free end of each brace and attach the stake to the brace.

Post level

Photo 2:3 Rip a 22½° bevel on one edge of a 2 × 4 to prepare the stock for cutting the blocking that's attached to the posts. A portable table saw is a perfect tool for performing this operation on-site.

TWO: Build the undercarriage

The undercarriage of the gazebo is composed of the posts and the joists that support the floor platform. The posts must be installed so all the inside faces would be perpendicular to straight lines if they were extended out from the center of the gazebo. The 4 × 4 posts are mounted to the footings with metal post anchors that are attached to the J-bolts set in the footings. The lengths of the posts will vary according to the above-grade height you want for the floor platform. The best bet is to let the posts run overlong; you can trim the tops after the deck is constructed.

To begin setting up the posts, mount all the metal post anchors. Line up the anchors and fasten them to the J-bolts with washers and nuts *(See Photo 2:1)*. Erect the first two posts on directly opposite sides of the gazebo. Attach them to the post anchors by driving joist hanger nails through the predrilled holes in the anchor tabs. Attach a pair of 2 × 4 braces to each post with deck screws, then drive stakes and loosely attach the free ends of the braces to the stakes. Using a post level as a guide, level and plumb each post then tighten the brace screws at the stakes to hold the post in position *(See Photo 2:2)*. You can go ahead and erect all eight posts at this point, but you might be better off putting them up in pairs as you hang the joists—they can create a bit of a traffic jam in the working area.

Before attaching the joist hangers to the posts, you'll need to cut and install 2 × 4 blocking to each post at joist height. The blocking creates a surface for attaching the joist hangers and also creates nailing surfaces for attaching the rim joist boards. To make the blocking pieces, bevel-rip 2 × 4s so one edge is 22½° *(See Photo 2:3)*. We used a

Square edge of blocking faces inward

Beveled edge of blocking faces outward

Photo 2:4 Cut 7¼-in.-long pieces of the beveled blocking stock and attach one to each side of one post. The tops should be flush with the layout marks for the top of the joist. Use 3 in. deck screws to fasten the blocking.

Photo 2:5 Use a water level to transfer a joist layout mark to the post opposite the post you attached the blocking to. Water levels are very accurate tools for setting layout lines with consistent heights. Unlike strings and line levels, there is no risk that a water level will sag and cause errant readings.

Photo 2:6 Nail double joist hangers to the inside faces of the two opposite posts. Position each hanger so the top of the doubled joist that will rest in it will be flush with the joist layout lines. Use joist hanger nails to attach the joist hangers: they have much greater shear strength than deck screws. Tıp: *Slip two cutoff joist pieces into the hanger as a guide for positioning it.*

Joist layout line

portable table saw to make this cut. Before installing the blocking, draw layout lines for the tops of the joists (and blocking) on each post. If the building site is not level, find the post at the highest point and begin there. Measure up 9¼ in. from the top of the footing and scribe a reference mark for the top of the joist. Attach a piece of blocking on each side of the post so the tops are flush with the reference line. The beveled edges should face outward and follow the octagonal outline of the gazebo *(See Photo 2:4)*.

Use a line level and mason's strings (or better yet, a water level) to transfer the joist height mark to the other post *(See Photo 2:5)*. Attach blocking to the sides of each post at the joist height marks.

Attach a double joist hanger to the two opposing posts. The hangers should be positioned so the joist will be flush with the joist lines when installed (set pieces of scrap joist material into each hanger for reference). Attach the hangers with joist hanger nails *(See Photo 2:6)*.

The joist structure is built by hanging a doubled, full-width joist between two opposite posts: all other joist members depend on the doubled joist for interior support. Cut two full-length joists (See Cutting List) and screw them together face to face (you may want to use construction adhesive as well). Hang the first joist *(See Photo 2:7)*.

Cut and hang the single joists that fit at right angles against the doubled joist *(See Photo 2:8)*. Attach joist hangers to the posts and on the doubled joist for support.

The four remaining joists are attached to blocking that's inserted between perpendicular joists at the center of the gazebo undercarriage. Cut blocking pieces to length (See Cutting List), with 45° miters at each end. Attach the blocking

Photo 2:7 Set the full-diameter-length doubled joist into the two opposing double joist hangers (you'll want a helper for this). Check to make sure the doubled joist is level (shim the low end if it is not), then secure it with joist hanger nails driven through the flanges of the joist hangers.

pieces between the installed joists *(See Photo 2:9).* When all four pieces are installed, measure out from each blocking piece to the rim joist, at a right angle, to find the required length of the remaining joists. Subtract about ¼ in. from each joist length measurement to allow for movement.

Cut the remaining joists to length and hang them with joist hangers *(See Photo 2:10).*

Cut and install the rim joists. The rim joists extend from post to post, forming the outer perimeter of the floor platform. The ends of each rim joist are cut at a bevel. Two beveled rim joist boards butt together to form a 45° angle at each post.

In an ideal world, all the rim joists would be the same length and would have the same bevel angle, so you could cut them all at once without changing the set-up on your saw. But in real life, the joists probably will vary in length and bevel angle. To mark the 2 × 8 rim joists for cutting, tack a 2 × 8 to two adjacent posts. Make sure the beveled post blocking is flush against the back face of the rim

Photo 2:8 Install posts, then hang the longer half-joists that are attached directly to the doubled joist, using single joist hangers. By accurately transferring the joist layout line from one of the doubled joist posts, you'll ensure that the tops of the rest of the joists all are level with one another.

Photo 2:9 Miter-cut pieces of 2 × 8 to fit between joists at the hub area of the under-carriage. The blocking creates flat, square surfaces for hanging the rest of the joists. Attach the blocking by tacking it in place with deck screws, then toe-nailing with 16d common nails.

Photo 2:10 Hang the four shorter half-joists between the posts and the joist hub blocking with single joist hangers. Once all of the joists are installed, you can go ahead and remove the braces supporting the posts.

2:11

Photo 2:11 Mark the rim joist stock for cutting by tacking boards in place, then extending a line from the midpoint of each post to the board. Use a square (a speed square is shown here) to extend the cutting line.

Photo 2:12
Nail the rim joist in place with 16d casing nails. Angle the nails toward the miter joint between the rim joists to help draw the joint together.

2:12

joist, and that the ends of the rim joist extend past the blocking by a couple of inches on each end. Use a speed square or framing square to extend a cutting line at each end of the rim joist *(See Photo 2:11)*. The cutting line should start at the midpoint of the post face and extend out at a right angle. Mark each end of the rim joist, remove it and cut it (set your circular saw or table saw blade angle to match the angle of the cutting line on each joist board).

Cut and attach two rim joists, using 16d casing nails. *(See Photo 2:12)*. Install the rest of the rim joist boards one at a time.

NOTE: Arrange for inspection of the framing before installing decking.

THREE: Install the decking

Because the decking is the part of the floor that "shows," you'll want to take extra care when you install the boards. The deck will have a nicer, neater appearance if you strike a chalkline across the boards where they fall across joists

BARK SIDE UP OR BARK SIDE DOWN?

The subject of which deck board face should face up is currently under evaluation. Traditionally, deckbuilders have always installed boards with the bark side facing up, presuming that if the boards cup from exposure to moisture the cupping will be directed against the joist, preventing the surface of the deck from becoming uneven. But some industry experts assert that modern kiln-drying methods alter the character of the wood enough to reverse the direction of the cupping, so the boards actually cup toward the bark side. The best advice is to ask your lumber distributor which method they recommend.

and use the lines as guides to keep the fasteners in neat rows.

If you want to apply a wood preservative or another protective finish to the substructure or to the undersides of the deck boards, it's not a bad idea to apply it before attaching the decking (See pages 16 to 17).

The floor platform for our gazebo is decked with 5/4 × 6 in. (nominal) cedar deck boards. Because of the configuration of the platform framing, the decking is installed in a concentric, octagonal pattern. Study the drawing *Plan View-Floor Platform* on page 24. Note that the ends of the deck boards are mitered at 22½°. Each board extends from the centerline of one joist to the centerline of the adjacent joist. Also note that the outermost decking boards need to be notched to fit around the posts.

Snap chalklines along the centerlines of all the joist tops for reference when measuring for and installing the deck boards.

Begin installing deck boards at

Photo 3:1 Measure the distance from the outer post face to the edge of the rim joist joint, then add ¼ in. (for overhang) to that distance. Use this measurement to lay out the front cut of the notch you'll need to make in the deckboard to fit around the post.

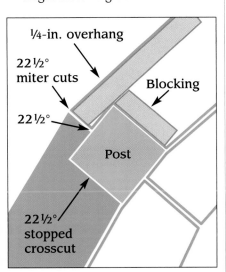

Deck board notching detail: The outer-ring deck boards must be notched to fit around the posts. Each deck board is mitered at 22½° to form 45° joints. A 22½° stopped crosscut that parallels the end miter cut is made to form one edge of each notch. The other sides are cut into the mitered ends, also at a 22½° angle, to follow the front post edges.

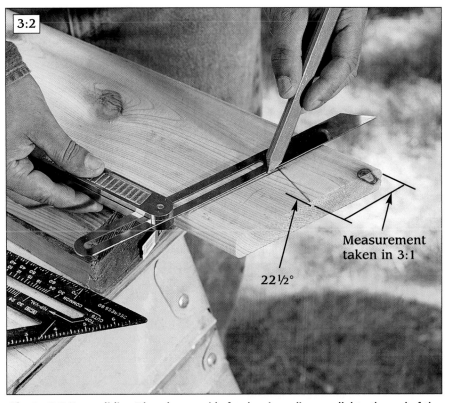

Photo 3:2 Use a sliding T-bevel as a guide for drawing a line parallel to the end of the deck board. The parallel line, scribed 1¾ in. in from the end of the board, defines the edge of the cutout area for notching the deck board to fit around the post.

the perimeter of the floor platform and work your way around the gazebo, toward the center, mitering the ends of the adjoining boards so they are flush and the edges are aligned. First, cut a 22½° miter at one end of an outer ring deck board. A power miter saw is the best tool for this job (many have positive stops at 22½°), but make a test cut first, then butt the cut ends together and check to make sure they form a 45° angle.

Mark the cutout lines for the notch that will fit around one end post (See *Illustration,* previous page). Start by measuring straight out from the midpoint of the post at the rim joist height *(See Photo 3:1).* The edge of the measuring tool should follow the rim joist joint. Add ¼ in. to establish the recess of the cutout edge from the outer edge of the deck board (the deck board edges should overhang the outer rim joist by ¼ in. all around). With a protractor

DRILL DRIVER TIP OPTIONS

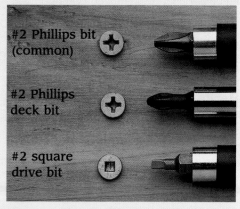

#2 Phillips bit (common)

#2 Phillips deck bit

#2 square drive bit

Three primary drill/driver bit styles are available for driving deck screws. A common #2 Phillips bit will easily drive deck screws through cedar or redwood decking without a pilot hole, but you may want to drill pilots if installing treated lumber. Specialty deck bits feature a hardened tip to withstand the torque that develops when you drive a screw through treated decking or 2× framing members. Square-drive screws are considerably more expensive than Phillips head screws, but they're less prone to stripping.

Photo 3:3 Cut out the notches in the outer ring of deck boards so they'll fit around the posts.

Photo 3:4 Cut the deck boards one at a time to fit between the joists, then attach them with 2½ in. deck screws driven through the deck boards and into the joists. Try to keep the screw heads aligned over the joist. Drill pilot holes when driving screws near the edge of a board.

or T-bevel, extend a cutting line into the end of the deck board at a 22½° angle.

From the outer corner of the mitered deck board end, measure in 1¾ in. (half the post width). Extend a cutting line from this mark to intersect with the first cutout line *(See Photo 3:2)*. Cut out the notch with a jig saw *(See Photo 3:3)*.

Cut and notch the other end of the deck board to fit around the post at the opposite end of the opening. Attach the board to the rim joists with 2½ in. deck screws. TIP: *When driving screws close to board ends, drill pilot holes first.* Fill in the remaining outer-ring (notched) deck boards, striving for tight miter joints between deck boards. Then, cut and install boards for the inner rings—you may need to make small relief cuts in the second-ring boards to accommodate the inside edges of the post. To cut the inner-ring boards, begin by mitering one end of a board at 22½°, then lay the board in position and mark the point where each board falls over the midpoint of the joist. Use your T-bevel to extend cutting lines from the end mark. NOTE: *While the mitered ends should fit together tightly, leave a ⅛ in. gap between parallel deck board edges: use 16d common nails as spacers.*

Install the rest of the deck boards *(See Photo 3:4)*. When you reach the "hub" of the platform, cut and install an octagonal fill piece to complete the deck board installation.

FOUR: Install the roof supports

Rafters resting atop the posts support the gazebo roof. The rafters are secured to the posts with battens that extend up along the sides of the post and overlap the rafters. Blocking is needed to fill the gaps between the battens

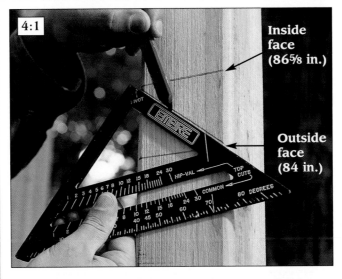

Photo 4:1 Scribe cutoff lines on the posts. Since you've made a painstaking effort to ensure that the joists are level, you can simply measure up from the decking 84 in. on the outside face of each post and 86⅝ in. on the inside face, then connect the points with a straightedge on each side.

Inside face (86⅝ in.)

Outside face (84 in.)

Photo 4:2 Working from a ladder, trim off each post at the cutoff line. Because of the thickness of the 4 × 4 stock, you'll need to make a cut from each side to clear the cut. Trim off most of the excess first to prevent the cutoff piece from breaking off and splintering.

Photo 4:3 Set up a table saw (we used a portable model on the job site) to chamfer the edges of a 6 × 6 block at each corner, creating the octagonal hub. With the blade set at 45°, measure out toward the fence 3⅝ in. from the point where the blade will contact the workpiece. Lock the fence in position.

and the rafter, since the posts are much thicker than the rafters. The rafters are cut from 2 × 6 stock, the filler blocks from 5/4 decking, and the battens from 2 × 4s. Depending on the actual dimensions of the lumber you use, you may need to install shims between the the fillers and the rafters (if the 5/4 decking is too thick for the opening, use 1× stock and shims).

The first task in creating the roof support system is to trim the posts to length, at an angle matching the roof pitch. Since the gazebo floor is level, you can measure the same distance up each post to mark it for cutting (no need to use a line level or a water level). The roof pitch is 9-in-12. Rather than get-ting caught up in trying to use a protractor, try this simple approach: Measure 84 in. up from the floor and scribe a line across the outside face of the post. Measure 86⅝ inches up the inside face of the post, and scribe a line across that face. Now, scribe angled lines across the post sides that connect the two points. Set the sliding T-bevel to the angled line scribed on the first post, and use the bevel to mark the mitered cutting lines on the remaining seven posts (See Photo 4:1). Trim the posts along the cutting lines (See Photo 4:2). A circular saw will yield the straight-est cut for most people, but you could use a reciprocating saw or a hand saw instead.

The center of the roof frame is an octagonal wood hub with faces wide enough to support the rafters. Since the hub needs to have a diameter of 3⅝ in., it must be formed from a 6 × 6 post. Chamfer off the corners of a post section so it is octagonal. A table saw is the best tool for this task. Position the rip fence so the blade tilts away from it. Adjust the fence so it is 3⅝ in. from the blade. Now, tilt the saw blade away from the fence at a 45° angle. Double-check to make sure the cut will start the correct distance from the fence (See Photo 4:3). Guide the block along the fence to trim off all four corners (See Photo 4:4). Because you'll need to remove the saw blade

Photo 4:4 With your table saw blade set at 45°, trim off all four corners of a piece of 6 × 6 stock to make the hub for the roof structure. Lay out the cuts so the uncut faces of the octago-nal hub will be 2¼ in. wide. Cut the hub to length.

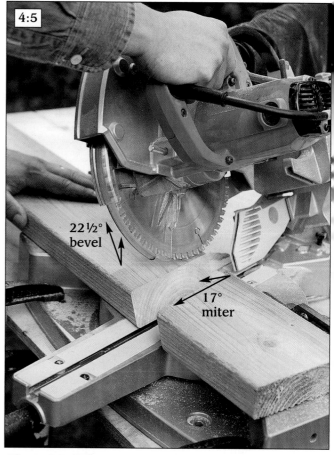

22½° bevel

17° miter

Photo 4:5 Make compound miter cuts at the lower rafter ends. Set the saw to cut a 22½° miter, then tilt the blade to cut a 17° bevel. Align each workpiece on the saw bed so the blade will exit halfway through the thickness of the board. Cut all eight rafter ends before changing the saw setup.

guard to make these cuts, use extra care as you work. Cut the post section to length to make the hub.

Lay out and cut the rafters, referring to the drawing *Rafter Pattern* on page 25. Note that the top end of each rafter is miter-cut to join the hub but has a square face to seat against the hub. The bottom end of the rafter is mitered at a different angle than the top. It is also beveled from both sides, forming a point (these cuts are *compound miter cuts*). The bevels create flat surfaces for the fascia boards to seat against. Because the bottom rafter ends are much trickier to cut than the tops, cut them first, then cut the rafters to length by making a simple miter cut at the top of each board.

Set up your miter saw to make the first compound miter cut at the bottom end of each rafter. The miter angle should be 17°, and the bevel angle is 22½°. Cut one side of all eight rafter bottoms *(See Photo 4:5).* To make the second bevel cut on the other side of each rafter bottom, keep the saw set up for a 22½° bevel the same direction, but swing it 17° to the opposite side of the zero point. With the cut side of the board facing down, position a rafter so the saw blade will exit the board midway through its thickness, resulting in a point that extends the full width of the rafter end and has symmetrical sides *(See Photo 4:6).* Make the bottom-end double bevels on each rafter.

The filler blocks are mitered at the top and bottom to follow the lines of the rafters. We used cutoff pieces of deck boards, ripped to 3½ in. wide, to make the fillers. The 5⁄4 (nominal) deck boards were actually exactly 1 in. thick, so attaching one on each side of the rafter extended the rafter width from 1½ in. to 3½ in.—the exact width of a 4 × 4 post. Because all the strips are cut to the same size and

4:6

Photo 4:6 Remove the rafter, swing the saw to 17° on the other side of the zero point, turn the workpiece over, align it with the blade and make the other side of the cut (keep the bevel at the same 22½° angle as the first cut. The peak of the resulting two-sided cut should fall at the midpoint of the rafter. Cut all eight rafters, then cut each to length with a simple 17° miter at the high end.

4:7

37° miter

6½ in.

Stopblock

Photo 4:7 Cut filler blocks to fill the gaps between the rafters and the sides of the posts that occur when the rafters are set and centered on the posts. Rip 1-in.-thick stock to 3½ in. (we used a 5⁄4 deck board), then cut off pieces with the saw set for a 37° miter cut. The edges of the filler blocks should be 6½ in. long (a stopblock will help you cut more accurately and quickly).

4:8

Photo 4:8 Cut the 2 × 4 battens that are attached over the joints between the posts and rafter/fillers to secure the connection. All 16 battens are mitered at the top at 37°. The battens that fit over the screen openings are 24 in. long and beveled at 45° at the bottoms. The two that get attached at the top of the door opening are square-cut to 5⅛ in. at the bottom.

at the same angle, the fastest way to produce them is to attach a stopblock to the table of your miter saw *(See Photo 4:7)*. Set the saw for a 37° cut and set the stopblock so the edges of the blocks will be 6½ in. long. You'll need 16 filler blocks.

The 2 × 4 battens lap the rafter/post joints on each side. The 14 regular battens are 24 in. long. To allow clearance for the door framing, the battens in the door opening area are square-cut to 5⅛ in. long. Bevel-cut the 14 regular battens at 45° on the bottoms for appearance. Then miter-cut the tops of all 16 battens at 37° to follow the roof slope line *(See Photo 4:8)*.

To assemble the roof frame, lag-screw the rafters to the hub and sandwich the rafters between the filler blocks and battens atop the posts: the filler blocks are attached to the rafters, then lag bolts are driven through the battens and filler blocks and the rafters. The tricky part is getting the first three rafters mounted on their posts and attached to the hub. Once this is done, the framework will be self-supporting, and you can work in a straightforward manner.

One reasonable approach at the beginning is to attach two rafters to the hub before lifting them up onto the posttops. Working on the ground, toe-nail two opposing rafters to the hub. The tops of the rafters should be flush with the top of the hub. To reinforce the joints, drill a counterbored pilot hole for a 5/16 × 4-

4:9

Photo 4:9 Attach two opposing rafters to the hub while the parts are still on the ground. Toe-nail the rafters to the hub to hold them in place. Make sure they're centered on the hub face, flush with the top and plumb. Reinforce each joint by driving a 5/16 × 4 in. lag screw through the rafter and into the hub.

4:10

Photo 4:10 Raise the rafter/hub assembly and balance it on two opposite posts. Toe-nail each rafter end to the post tops with two 16d nails per side to hold the assembly in place. Don't install the battens and fillers yet: wait until all rafters are positioned so you can make adjustments if needed.

Photo 4:11 Install the rest of the rafters, toe-nailing or screwing them toe-nail style to the hub and the post. Inspect to make sure all the bottom end overhangs are equal and the rafters are evenly spaced, plumb and flush against the hub faces and the post tops. Secure all rafters at the top with one lag screw apiece.

Photo 4:12 After nailing or screwing a filler strip to each rafter (the bottoms of the fillers should rest on the posts and the sides should be flush), install the battens. Tack them in place with nails, then drill two counterbored guide holes for bolts through each batten and into the rafter. Drive another pair of guide holes into the post.

in. lag screw (with washer) and drive one lag through each rafter, about 2 in. down from the top, and into the the hub (See Photo 4:9).

Set up sturdy stepladders (See page 9) next to two opposite posts. With a helper, lift the two-rafters-and-hub assembly onto the posts and adjust it so the overhang is equal on both posts (See Photo 4:10). The rafters should be centered on the posts. Toe-nail each side of each rafter to the post below with 16d common nails or 3- to 4-in. deck screws, making sure the fastener head is countersunk. These alone should hold the assembly in place and allow you to move one of the stepladders under the hub and the other to a new post. Toe-nail or screw the rest of the rafters in position (See Photo 4:11). Check to make sure all the rafters overhang the posts equally and are plumb. Drive a lag screw through each rafter top and into the hub.

Attach the filler blocks and battens. So they don't interfere with the roof sheathing, the tops of these parts should be 1 in. below the tops of the rafters. Nail the filler block to the rafters first, then tack the battens in position. Drill counterbored pilot holes for $\frac{3}{8} \times 6\frac{1}{2}$-

in. carriage bolts (See Photo 4:12). Insert a pair of bolts through each batten and into the rafter. Attach washers and nuts and tighten (See Photo 4:13). Make sure the bottoms of the short battens in the door opening are at the same height (See Photo 4:14).

Cut and attach the fascia boards. Use $\frac{5}{4}$ deck boards for the fascia. These extend from rafter-end to rafter-end, enclosing the perimeter of the roof and giving it a finished appearance. The ends of each fascia board must be cut with a compound angle so they seat tightly to the rafters and to the adjacent boards. The miter angle for the end cuts is $22\frac{1}{2}°$. For this gazebo, a 10° bevel accounted for the inward cant of the rafter ends: but you should measure the amount your rafter ends cant in from vertical to make sure the compound cut is correct for your project. Cut the fascia boards (you'll need to change your saw setup for each board end. Attach the fascia boards with 10d finish (casing) nails (See Photo 4:15). If you're concerned about the small black marks that can be created by galvanized metal on cedar (See page 12), use aluminum nails for this relatively visible joint.

Photo 4:13 Attach washers and nuts to the 3/8 × 6½-in. carriage bolts to complete the rafter/post connections.

Photo 4:14 Attach the shorter, square-bottom battens to the posts that frame the door opening.

Photo 4:15 Cut fascia boards to cover the rafter ends and nail them in place with 10d nails. Measure the inward angle of the rafter ends—ours canted in at 10°—and combine that bevel angle with a 22½° miter angle to make the compound miters cut on each end of each board.

FIVE: Build the roof

We installed fiberglass 3-tab shingles over ¾ in. exterior sheathing on this gazebo. The size and configuration of the roof allows you to cut two pie-wedge-shaped segments from each 4 × 8 sheathing sheet. Choose sheathing that has at least one presentable face: it will be visible from inside the gazebo.

Check the dimensions of your roof frame to confirm the sheathing dimensions shown in the Cutting List on page 23. The roof should be constructed of eight wedge-shaped pieces of plywood sheathing, each of which covers one section of the roof. The wedges should meet in a point at the top of the roof, but leave a ¼ in. gap between sheathing boards. Lay out the sheathing pieces on full sheets of plywood. To make sure the angles of the triangular shape are correct, start measuring in a corner and mark the base (low) end measurement. Measure and mark the midpoint of the base on the edge of the plywood. Use a framing square to mark a perpendicular line at the midpoint, then extend that line up toward the peak of the triangle. Mark the length of the sheathing piece on the line, then draw cutting lines to the corner and to the endpoint of the base line. Cut out the shape with a circular saw. Test the fit of the sheathing piece to make sure the edges fall over rafter and fascia locations. If it fits correctly, use the first piece as a template for laying out the other seven pieces. Cut all eight sheathing pieces *(See Photo 5:1)*.

Attach the sheathing. We used a pneumatic nailer *(See Photo 5:2)*, but you could use deck screws or 10d galvanized common nails instead. Cut and install the drip-edge molding next, using roofing nails (if your drip edge is aluminum, be sure to use aluminum nails). The proper approach here is to cut wedges out of the flange that overlays the sheathing so you can bend the material to follow the roof-edge contour. The end of one strip should overlap the end of its neighbor by about 1 in., and joints between pieces should fall over a straight run, not at the seam.

Staple building paper onto the sheathing (local codes in the area this gazebo was installed in required 30# building paper). Begin attaching the building paper at the eaves and work your way toward the peak of the roof *(See Photo 5:3)*. Use the reference lines printed on the building paper as a guide for aligning pieces. Higher courses should overlap lower courses by 2 in., and each piece should overlap the adjoining ridges by 6 in. Trim off any paper that extends past the front edge of the drip edge.

Lay a shingle starter course all the way around the eave edge of the roof. The shingles in the starter course should be turned upside-down so the tabs are on the high side. The exposed edges of the shingles should overhang the drip edge by ⅜ in. all around. Also make sure adjoining shingles are square. The end shingles should overlap the seams between roof sections *(See Photo 5:4)*. Drive one roofing nail near the top of each tab. Make sure all nail heads are in areas that will

Photo 5:1 Lay out and cut the wedge-shaped roof sheathing from plywood sheets. You should be able to cut two sheathing pieces from each 4 × 8 plywood sheet. Test the first piece to make sure it fits before you cut the rest of the pieces. Note that there should be a gap of around ⅛ in. between sheets when installed, to allow for expansion.

Photo 5:2 Attach the roof sheathing to the rafters. We used a pneumatic nail gun, but 2 in. deck screws or #10d ring-shank nails will also do the job.

Photo 5:3 Attach drip-edge molding to the bottom edge of the roof deck. Make release cuts in the molding flange so it can be bent around corners without buckling. Then, staple building paper to the roof deck, starting at the bottom.

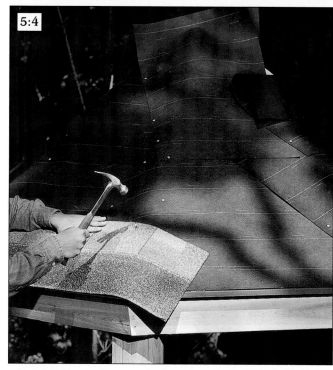

Photo 5:4 Install the shingle starter course. The shingles in this row are installed upside down. Overlap the sheathing seams and make sure adjacent shingles are aligned and flush to one another.

Photo 5:5 Install the first course of right-side-up shingles. Position the shingles so the slots point down. Drive one roofing nail above each slot, and stagger the seams so they don't align with the starter course seams.

Photo 5:6 Work your way up the section, making sure to stagger shingle tabs and slots. Overlap the seams between roof sections, then trim off the ends after finishing each course. Shingle all the sections.

be covered by the next course of shingles. Don't forget to peel the cellophane strip off the back of each shingle before you apply it. TIP: *Run a bead of asphalt roof cement near the eave to bond the starter course to the building paper.*

Install a course of shingles directly over the starter course *(See Photo 5:5)*, but with this course, position the shingles so the tabs are lower (standard installation). Also, shift the shingles over by one-half tab so the slots and seams are not aligned. Drive one roofing nail about an inch above each slot.

After each course, trim the shingles at the seams between roof sections. This will prevent conspicuous bulging when the ridge caps are applied. Shingle all the way up to the peak *(See Photo 5:6)*. The roof sections on most gazebos are small enough that trying to use the traditional shingling method of staggering slots by half-tab thicknesses may not work out well. In such a case, simply adjust the shingles as you start each course so the seams are not aligned. Try to preserve some uniformity in the stagger pattern.

When the roof is shingled all the way up to the peak, go back to the ridges and install "ridge caps" to cover the seams between roof sections. To make a ridge cap, cut a shingle into thirds. Starting at the bottom of the roof slope, fold a ridge cap across the ridge and nail it in place. Work up the ridge, installing the ridge caps—make sure to cover the nail heads in the lower shingles— *(See Photo 5:7)*. When all the ridge caps are installed, trim the bottom edges to follow the line of the regular shingles.

Trim the non-mineralized backing off of a ridge cap shingle and fit it over the peak. You'll need to cut a small slot in each side of the peak cap shingle so it can be folded to fit *(See Photo 5:8)*. Nail the peak shingle down securely and cover the exposed nailheads with roof cement.

Photo 5:7 Cut ridge cap shingles and install them over the ridges between roof sections, starting at the bottom and working your way up.

Photo 5:8 Slit a ridge cap shingle so it can be folded without tearing, then tack it over the peak of the roof. Depending on how much of the peak is exposed on your roof, this may take more than one shingle. Trial and error is the best method for solving the issue. Nail the shingle down and cover the nailheads with roof cement.

Photo 6:1 Cut out the balusters on your band saw or with a jig saw after laying out the pattern. We ganged two together at a time to speed up this time-consuming task.

Photo 6:2 Cut slots in the top and bottom rails to house the ends of the balusters. A dado-blade set mounted in your table saw is the perfect tool for this task.

Photo 6:3 Measure to determine how long to make the rails for each opening. Clamp the 1 × 4 battens to the posts first and measure from the inside faces of the battens.

SIX: Install railings & trim

The railings and trim are two focal points that give this gazebo its elegant appearance, so we decided to invest a bit of time and energy in creating them. If this seems like too much work, you can buy ready-made deck-railing balusters. In fact, you can also purchase railing stringers and cap rails in premilled form, eliminating the need to rip and slot the top and bottom rails on a table saw, as we do here.

Using a power miter saw with a stopblock, cut 1 × 4s to make the balusters. Make a cardboard template using the *Baluster Pattern* on page 25 as a guide. Stack two or three boards face-to-face and bind them with masking tape. Trace the pattern, then cut out the shape on the entire stack *(See Photo 6:1)*.

Make the top and bottom rails. The rails that form the top and bottom of the railing structures are made from 2 × 4s ripped to 2½ in. wide on a table saw (some lumber yards carry 2 × 3s). All rails are machined with ¾ in. wide by ½ in. deep slots, cut lengthwise, to accept the ends of the balusters. Use a dado-blade set mounted in your table saw *(See Photo 6:2)*.

The rails are mitered at 22½° on the ends to match the angles of the post sides. Then they are attached to 1 × 4 battens which are fastened to the posts. After the slots are cut, cut and clamp 1 × 4 battens to the posts in each railing opening. Measure between the battens to determine the required lengths of the top and bottom rails *(See Photo 6:3)*. Miter-cut the rails to fit.

To assemble the rail frames, lay a rail slot-side-up on your worksurface. Mark the midpoint of the railing, then mark a point ³/₁₆ in. from the midpoint. Lay a bead of construction adhesive in the slot and insert a baluster so the edge is aligned with the second mark *(See Photo 6:4)*. Using a ⅜ in. dowel as a spacer, insert the rest of the balusters. It is important to maintain even spacing between balusters, so let "leftover" space in the slot fall between the end balusters and the posts. Drive a pair of finish nails through the rail to hold each baluster in position (we used a pneumatic pin nailer). Lay a bead of construction adhesive in the other rail and fit it over the free ends of the balusters *(See Photo 6:5)*. Check the assembly with a framing square and adjust as needed, then nail the second rail to the baluster ends. Attach the battens to the railing assembly so the tops are flush with the top railing *(See Photo 6:6)*. Construct all seven railing assemblies, custom-measuring for each.

Set the railing assemblies into the correct openings and attach them by nailing or screwing the battens to the posts. Cut cap rail from 5/4 deck boards. Each cap rail should fit between two posts, and the ends should be mitered to match the post angles (22½°). Attach the cap rail to the top rails of the railing assemblies with con-

Photo 6:4 Apply construction adhesive into the bottom rail slot (assemble one section at a time). Arrange the balusters in the slot using a ⅜-in. dowel as a spacer. Start in the middle and work toward the ends.

Photo 6:5 Apply construction adhesive in the top rail slot and fit the top rail over the free ends of the balusters. Use the midpoint mark on the rail to set the layout (a baluster should start ³⁄₁₆ in. on each side of the midpoint). Use a ⅜ in. dowel spacer to set the rest of the gaps (any overage can be picked up outside the end balusters). Drive a nail through each rail and into each baluster end.

Photo 6:6 With the railing section upside down, attach the 1 × 4 battens to each end of the section. The battens should be flush with the top of the top rail.

Photo 6:7 Insert the railing section into the opening and attach it by nailing through the battens and into the posts. Cut the cap rails to fit and attach with construction adhesive and 10d finish nails. Make and install all the railing sections.

Photo 6:8 Install the horizontal frieze boards at the top of each frame opening. Set the nailheads with a nailset. The board ends are mitered at 22½°.

Photo 6:9 Bevel the tops of the vertical frieze boards to follow the roof slope, then miter-cut the ends. Nail the vertical boards into the top of each opening.

Photo 6:10 Drive finish nails through the horizontal frieze boards and into the bottom edges of the vertical boards to draw the joint together.

Photo 6:12 Nail the corner brackets in place at the top corners of the screen frame openings, centered on the post battens. Don't install them in the door opening.

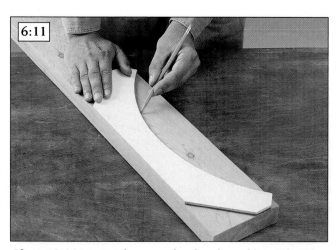

Photo 6:11 Lay out the corner brackets by making and tracing a hardboard template, according to the *Corner Bracket Pattern* shown on page 25.

struction adhesive, then toe-nail the ends to the posts with 10d casing nails *(See Photo 6:7).*

The primary trim parts on the gazebo are the corner brackets at the tops of the openings between posts, and frieze boards that are installed between the fascia and the underside of the roof on the interior of the gazebo. You'll need both horizontal and vertical frieze boards to box in the frieze area. Cut the horizontal boards first, mitering the ends to follow the post angles. The bottoms of these boards should be flush with the bottom edges of the fascia boards. Install the horizontal boards by toe-nailing them into the posts with finish nails *(See Photo 6:8).* Set the nailheads with a nailset throughout the frieze. The vertical boards are beveled on the ends and on the top edge to fit snugly between the horizontal frieze boards and the roof. Measure the opening and the bevel angles (they should be 22½° on the sides and 37° on the top), then cut the boards to fit with a jig saw or on your table saw. We needed to use 1 × 8 stock to fit the openings. Insert the vertical boards into the openings *(See Photo 6:9)* and secure them by nailing up through the horizontal boards with finish nails *(See Photo 6:10).*

Make a template for the corner brackets from cardboard or hardboard, using the pattern on page 25 as a guide. Lay the template onto a 2 × 6 and trace the pattern onto the board *(See Photo 6:11).* Cut out the shape with a jig saw or band saw. Make all 14 corner brackets.

Attach a corner bracket at each post opening (except the door opening), using casing or finish nails driven into pilot holes *(See Photo 6:12).* The brackets should be centered on the rafter-support battens.

Building Stairs

Generally, outdoor stairs are not as steep as indoor stairs, having proportionally wider treads and lower risers. The clear width between outer stringers should be at least 36 in.

To build a comfortable set of stairs, you'll need to establish a suitable rise-to-run ratio: *Rise* refers to the height between the steps; *run* refers to the depth of the step, minus any overhang. As a general rule for outdoor stairs, the tread width (run) in inches

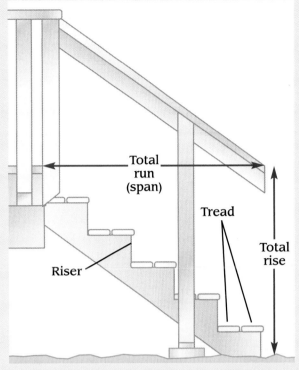

Designing stairs involves a little math and a little trial-and-error. The trick is to come up with a plan that has uniformly sized risers and treads that are in formation and terminate at a convenient location on the low end of the flight.

plus twice the step height (rise) in inches should equal 24 to 26 inches. For exterior stairs, the rise (vertical distance between treads) should be between 4½ in. and 7 in. The tread depth should be a minimum of 11 in. Building codes often dictate acceptable run/rise relationships. For most structures with decking, treads consist of two 2 × 6s, spaced ¼ in. apart, to create a tread run of 11¼ in. In this case, the formulas tell us that the riser height should be between 6½ and 7 in. This is the most common and useful outdoor step relationship.

The real trick to designing stairs comes when you try to actually incorporate the run and rise ratios into your design. By code, all stairs in a flight must have the same rise and run proportions (this is a safety issue: non-uniform sizing of stairs confuse our feet in a hurry and can easily cause injury from falls).

STRINGER BRACKETS

Stringer brackets, which work like joist hangers, cradle the bottom of the stringer and provide nailing flanges for attaching the stringers to the deck joists. They are a quick and convenient substitute for building stringers from scratch. Use 1¼-in. joist-hanger nails for fasteners.

Photo 7:1 Measure the total rise of the gazebo deck at the door opening to begin planning your stairs. Measure from the lowest point of ground outside the door opening.

Photo 7:2 Design and build your stairs (See previous page). Here, we buried a landscape timber at the foot of the stairs for support and rested the inside edge of the construction on the footings. A ledger attached to the rim joist keeps the staircase from pinching in, but is not attached to the staircase due to ground swell issues.

Photo 7:3 Use the same decking and amount of overhang to make the stair treads as were used on the gazebo deck.

SEVEN: Finishing touches

By now, your gazebo project is nearing completion and only a few optional finishing touches remain. Because the floor of the gazebo is raised by more than a foot, you'll need to provide a step at the doorway. You have several options, depending on how much distance there is between the floor and ground and a few other factors. The simplest solution is to attach a simple stair stringer bracket to the rim joist (See previous page). But we opted for a slightly more elegant approach.

Measure the distance from the ground to the top of the gazebo floor (called the stair *rise*) at the doorway opening *(See Photo 7:1)*. Design your stairs (See previous page). We chose to build a two-step box frame that is attached to the rim joist *(See Photo 7:2)*. We used deck boards to make the stair treads *(See Photo 7:3)*.

After the steps are installed is a good time to apply the finish to the gazebo, unless you're using a wood like cedar that is naturally moisture resistant and can be left untreated (See pages 14 to 15). We applied redwood stain with UV protection to the project.

Prepare the gazebo for the finish. Preparation steps include setting nailheads with a nailset (it's usually not that important to fill nail holes or screw holes with putty, but if you do, be sure to use a moisture-resistant exterior wood filler), sanding down any rough edges, and sanding out any footprints, stains or blemishes that would show up through the finish *(See Photo 7:4)*. We also hosed down the gazebo and let it dry before applying the redwood stain *(See Photo 7:5)*.

Just about every region of the country is plagued by some type of flying pest, be they gnats, mosquitoes, yellow jackets, blackflies or anything else. Consequently,

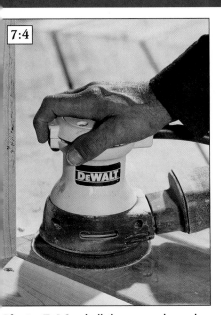

Photo 7:4 Sand all the exposed wood surfaces to prepare them for finishing (and to clean them after all the construction traffic).

Photo 7:5 Apply your finish of choice before installing the screen frames. We used semi-transparent redwood stain.

screens and a screen door may be in order for your gazebo. You can make a set that can be removed for winter storage, and it isn't hard for someone who's just constructed a gazebo.

Rip eight post battens to 1½ in. wide from 1× stock. Cut them to length to extend from floor to rafter. Apply finish. Snap a plumb chalkline on the inside face of each post, right down the center. Nail a batten to each post, centered on the chalkline (See Photo 7:6).

Each screen frame consists of two stiles and three rails. The object here is to make a simple frame upon which to stretch window screening. You don't want fat frame members impinging on the openness of the gazebo. Since the frame will be clipped to the posts and won't move, it doesn't have to be particularly stiff or rigid or wrack-resistant. The stiles and two of the rails therefore are cut from 1 × 2 stock. The third rail, the bottom one, is subject to inadvertent kicks and bumps from chair legs, so it is wider with enough strength to resist these indignities. Cut the

bottom rail from 1 × 4 stock.

To determine the required dimensions of each screen frame, measure straight across the opening from batten to batten (See Photo 7:7). It's a good idea to cut a stick to that length and test-fit it between all the battens, top and bottom. Subtract 3 in. from that measurement, and cut all the rails to that length. The stiles should be the same length as the battens.

In keeping with the simplicity objective, the frames are assembled with reinforced butt joints. Two 3-in. galvanized screws secure each joint. Lay out the stiles and set the rails between them. Obviously, the bottom rail (the wide one) is flush with the bottom end of the stiles, and the top rail flush with the stile tops. The middle rail should be at railing height. Pull the stiles tight against the rail ends and square up the assembly by measuring the diagonals (See Photo 7:8). Drill and countersink two pilot holes at each joint. Drive the screws. Remove the clamps. The process is the same for each of the seven frames needed.

Cut, but don't attach, molding to

Photo 7:6 Nail a mounting batten to the inside face of each post in each screen frame opening. Apply finish to the battens first and center them on a centerline on the post.

Photo 7:7 Measure between the post battens to determine the width of each screen frame. Subtract 3 in. to find the rail length. The stiles should be the same length as the post battens.

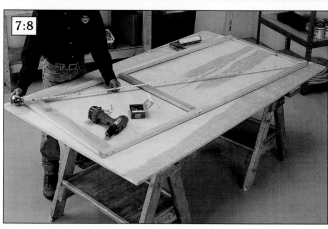

Photo 7:8 Cut the rails and stiles for each screen frame. Dry-fit the parts and check for square. Join the frames with butt joints reinforced with glue and 3-in. screws.

Photo 7:9 Roll out the window screening, set a frame on top of it, and trim it to rough length. Measure the length and cut the screening to that length for the rest of the frames.

Photo 7:10 Slip a 2 × 4 under each end of the frame and clamp the middle of the frame to your worksurface, creating a bow. Staple the screening to the top and bottom rails, then release the clamps to stretch the screening taut.

Photo 7:11 Staple the screening to the stiles and the middle rail. Try to keep the staples within the area that will be covered with the molding.

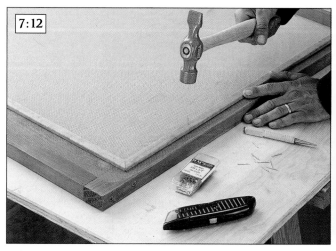

Photo 7:12 Miter-cut window stop molding to frame the screen opening and tack it to the frame, concealing the staples. Also tack molding over the middle rail.

surround the openings in the frame. These are to cover the edges of the screening and the staples that secure it. Use strips of astragal or bead molding, or simply thin flat strips—we used window stop molding. Assuming you will apply a finish to the frames, now is the time to do it.

When the finish is dry, attach the screening. To begin, cut the screening to length plus a few inches, using a utility knife. Spread out the screening and lay the frame on top of it. Keep the screen mesh as straight as possible and parallel to the frame edges. Trim the screening along the frame edges *(See Photo 7:9)*.

Turn the frame over and lay the screening on top. Staple the screening to the bottom rail. Start in the center and work toward the bottom corners of the frame, driving staples about 6 in. apart. Smooth the screening as you work to eliminate wrinkles. Keep the staples in a tidy line, so it will be easy to cover them with the molding in the next step. Place a 2 × 4 under each end of the frame and apply C-clamps at the center, forcing the frame into a concave bow. Stretch the screen to the top of the frame, pulling it taut. Drive a staple at the center of the top rail *(See Photo 7:10),* and work out to the corner, stapling every 6 in. The screening will now be stapled at the top and bottom, but not the sides.

Release the clamps, and the frame will spring back flat, stretching the screening nice and tight. Now drive staples along the two sides and across the middle rail *(See Photo 7:11).*

Nail the molding to the frames with brads or small finishing nails *(See Photo 7:12).* Trim off the excess screening *(See Photo 7:13).*

Attach a mitered wood strip to the molding side of each screen frame, flush with the top edge *(See Photo 7:14).* The mitered strips fill

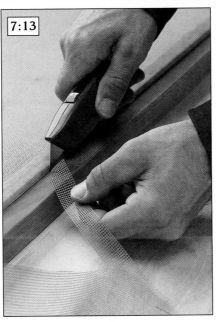

Photo 7:13 Trim off the excess screening next to the molding material with a utility knife.

Photo 7:14 Nail miter-cut filler strips to the top of each screen to fill the gaps next to the frieze boards.

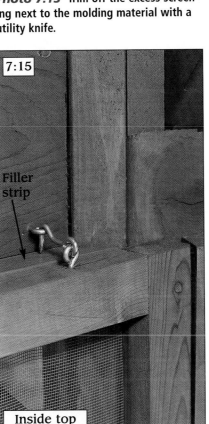

Filler strip

Inside top

Photo 7:15 Attach screw eyes to the frieze boards and attach eyebolts to each top corner of each window frame. Fit each screen frame into its opening and fasten it in place with the eyebolts.

Outside bottom

Photo 7:16 Use the same method to fasten the bottoms of the screen frames. The screw eyes are driven into the post battens.

Photo 7:17 Purchase a wood-frame screen door and hang it in the door opening, following the manufacturer's installation instructions. Set the door on wood shims when marking hinge locations.

Photo 7:18 Attach the hinges, making sure there is a slight gap between each side of the door and posts. Once the door is hung, install a door closer and handle/latch assembly.

the gap between the screens and the frieze inside the gazebo. To size the strips, set the screen in place and measure.

Attach screw eyes to the top and bottom edges of each screen, near the corners. Attach eyebolts to the frieze boards *(See Photo 7:15)* and to the post battens *(See Photo 7:16)* so they align with the screw eyes. Install the screens by hooking the screw eyes through the eyebolts.

Buy a wooden screen door, hinges, door closing hardware and a latch. You can make either of two choices when it comes to the door width. If the stiles of the door are wide enough, you can cut or plane a bevel on both of them so a 32-in.-wide door will fit between the posts. Or you can make some thin beveled strips to nail to the posts, squaring the opening, and use a 30-inch door. Whichever approach you take, the door should be hung so it opens out.

In a nutshell, the procedure is to stand the door in the opening. To get the proper clearance at the bottom, slip a couple of wood shims between the floor and the door. Allow a slight gap on the sides of the door as well. When the door is centered and shimmed, mount the hinges. This is a matter of holding the hinge in place and marking the mounting screw locations *(See Photo 7:17)*. Drill pilot holes. Screw the hinges to the screen door, then to the posts *(See Photo 7:18)*. Attach the door closing hardware and latch.

GATEWAY

A delightful hybrid between the pergola and the trellis,
this stunning gateway project transforms
a simple back yard into a magical garden.

Gateway Project: *A 3-step overview*

Build the gateway arches (60 to 64)

Build the trellises (65 to 70)

Assemble & install the gateway (71 to 74)

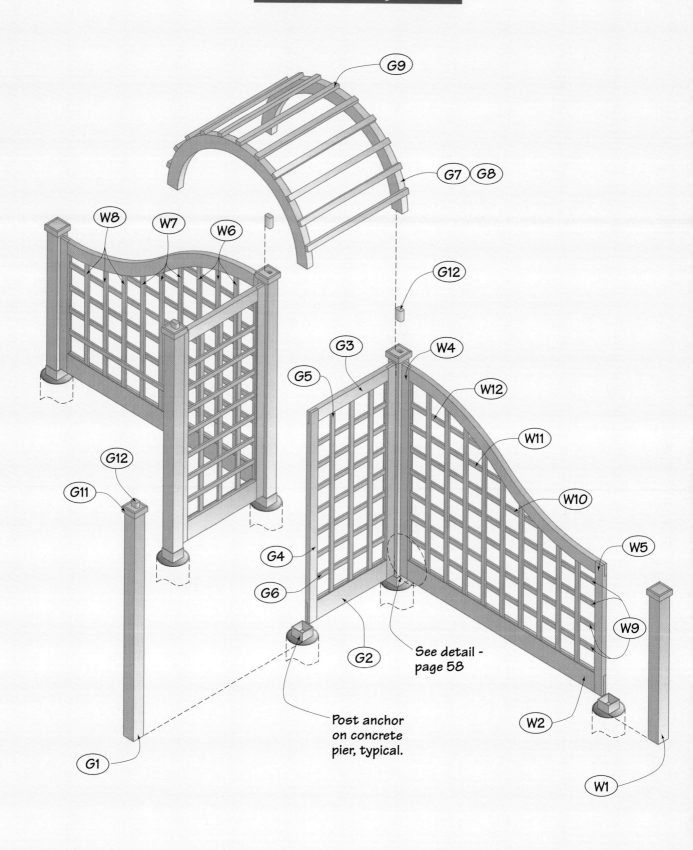

G9

G7 G8

W8 W7 W6

G12

G3 W4

G5 W12

G11 G12 W11

G4 W10

G6 W5

G2 W9

See detail -
page 58

G1

Post anchor
on concrete
pier, typical.

W2

W1

Cutting List

OVERALL DIMENSIONS (37″ × 196½ × 91½″)

KEY	PART NAME	QTY.	SIZE	MATERIAL
ARCHWAY				
G1	POST	4	3½ × 3½ × 66″	CEDAR (4 × 4)
G2	BOTTOM RAIL	2	1½ × 5½ × 29″	CEDAR (2 × 6)
G3	TOP RAIL	2	1½ × 3½ × 29″	CEDAR (2 × 4)
G4	STILE	4	1½ × 2½ × 61¼″	CEDAR (2 × 4)
G5	VERTICAL SLAT	6	½ × 1¼ × 54¼″	CEDAR (1 × 6)
G6	HORIZONTAL SLAT	14	½ × 1¼ × 26″	CEDAR (1 × 6)
G7	ARCH SEGMENT	18	1 × 5 × 16″	5/4 CEDAR DECK BOARD
G8	ARCH SEGMENT	4	1 × 5 × 8″	5/4 CEDAR DECK BOARD
G9	ARCH RUNG	11	1 × 1½ × 34½″	CEDAR (2 × 4)
G10	POST CAP	8	¾ × 3½ × 3½″	CEDAR
G11	MOLDING	16	½ × 1½ × 4½″	CEDAR (2 × scrap)
G12	LOOSE TENONS	4	1¼ × 2 × 3″	CEDAR
WING TRELLISES				
W1	END POST	2	3½ × 3½ × 42¾″	CEDAR (4 × 4)
W2	BOTTOM RAIL	2	1½ × 5½ × 69¾″	CEDAR (2 × 6)
W3	CREST RAIL	2	1½ × 8 × 74¾″	CEDAR (2 × 10)
W4	TALL STILE	2	1½ × 2½ × 61¼″	CEDAR (2 × 4)
W5	SHORT STILE	2	1½ × 2½ × 38″	CEDAR (2 × 4)
W6	VERTICAL SLAT	6	½ × 1¼ × 54″	CEDAR (1 × 6)
W7	VERTICAL SLAT	6	½ × 1¼ × 46¼″	CEDAR (1 × 6)
W8	VERTICAL SLAT	6	½ × 1¼ × 34¾″	CEDAR (1 × 6)
W9	HORIZONTAL SLAT	8	½ × 1¼ × 66¾″	CEDAR (1 × 6)
W10	HORIZONTAL SLAT	2	½ × 1¼ × 51¼″	CEDAR (1 × 6)
W11	HORIZONTAL SLAT	2	½ × 1¼ × 40¼″	CEDAR (1 × 6)
W12	HORIZONTAL SLAT	2	½ × 1¼ × 28⅜″	CEDAR (1 × 6)
W13	POST CAP	2	¾ × 3½ × 3½″	CEDAR
W14	MOLDING	8	½ × 1½ × 4½″	CEDAR (2 × scrap)
HARDWARE REQUIRED				
NAILS			¾″, 1¼″	STAINLESS STEEL
DECK SCREWS			#8 × 2½″	
CONSTRUCTION ADHESIVE				
WATERPROOF GLUE				
POST ANCHOR/STAKES		6	3½ × 3½ × 24″	STEEL

NOTICE: Part dimensions are based on ideal installation conditions. For best results, confirm measurements on actual project before cutting parts.

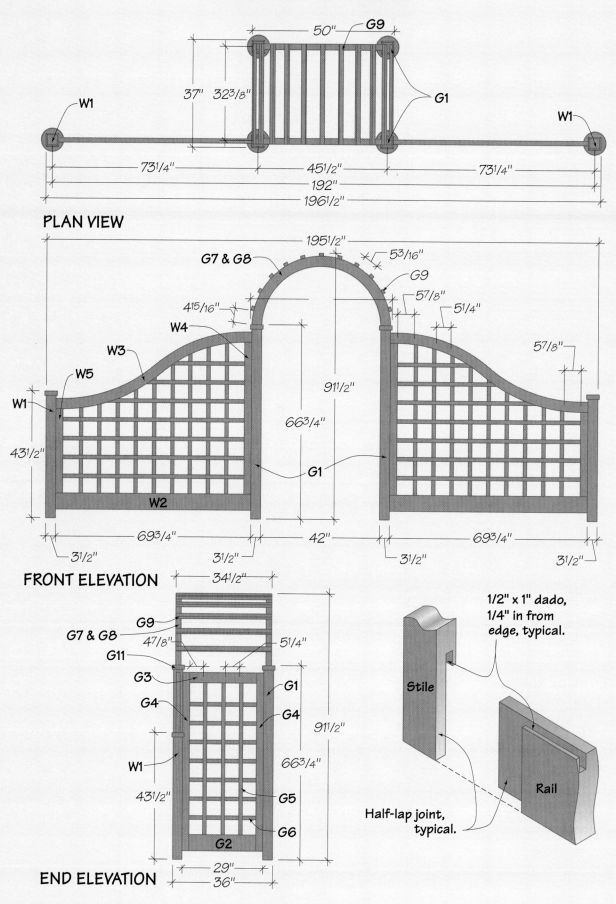

PLAN VIEW

50"

G9

37" 32³/₈"

G1

W1

W1

73¹/₄"   45¹/₂"   73¹/₄"

192"

196¹/₂"

195¹/₂"

G7 & G8

5³/₁₆"

G9

5⁷/₈"

4¹⁵/₁₆"

5¹/₄"

W4

W3

5⁷/₈"

W5

91¹/₂"

W1

66³/₄"

43¹/₂"

G1

W2

69³/₄"   42"   69³/₄"

3¹/₂"   3¹/₂"   3¹/₂"   3¹/₂"

FRONT ELEVATION

34¹/₂"

G9

G7 & G8

47/8"

5¹/₄"

G11

G3

G1

G4

G4

91¹/₂"

W1

66³/₄"

43¹/₂"

G5

G6

G2

29"

36"

END ELEVATION

1/2" x 1" dado, 1/4" in from edge, typical.

Stile

Rail

Half-lap joint, typical.

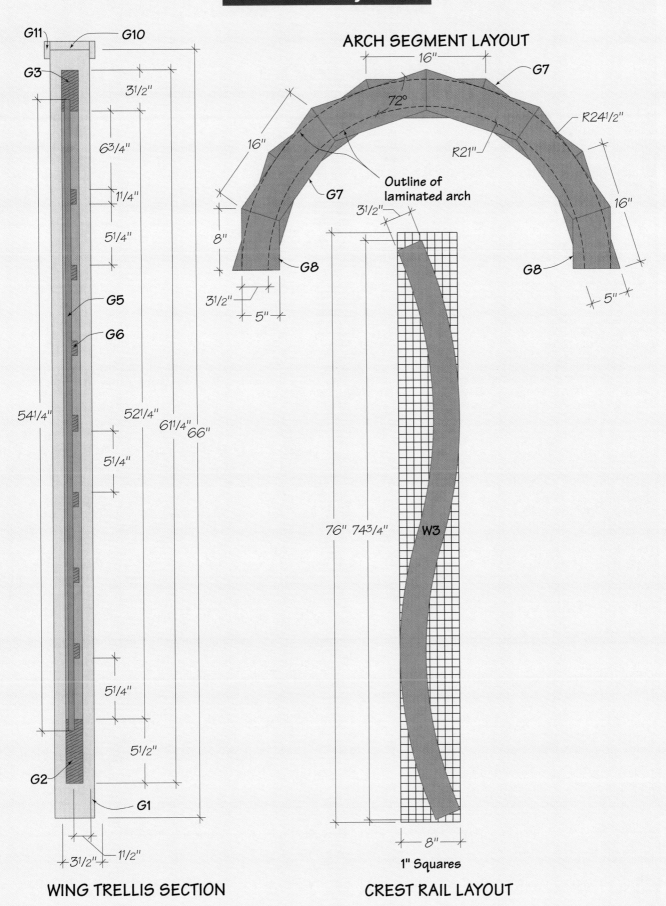

ARCH SEGMENT LAYOUT

G11
G10
G3
3¹/₂"
6³/₄"
1¹/₄"
5¹/₄"
G5
G6
54¹/₄"
52¹/₄"
61¹/₄"
66"
5¹/₄"
5¹/₄"
5¹/₂"
G2
G1
3¹/₂"
1¹/₂"

16"
G7
72°
16"
R24¹/₂"
R21"
Outline of
laminated arch
G7
8"
G8
3¹/₂"
5"
16"
G8
5"

3¹/₂"
76" 74³/₄" W3
8"

1" Squares

WING TRELLIS SECTION

CREST RAIL LAYOUT

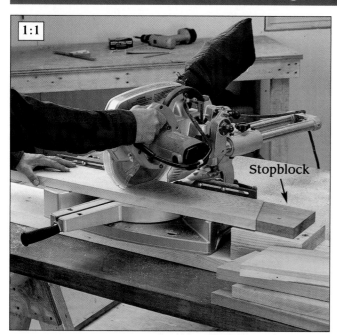

Photo 1:1 Miter-cut the overlapping board segments at a 72° angle to make the "bricklaid" blank that will be cut into the arch shape. A stopblock speeds up the process.

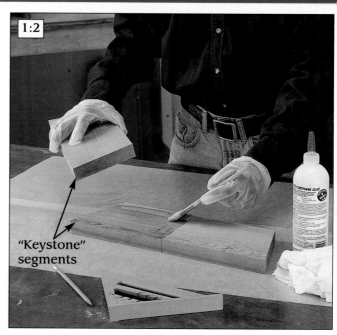

Photo 1:2 Apply glue up to the centerline on the face of one of the three "keystone" segments. Also apply glue to the mating face of another keystone segment, stopping at the centerline.

For a romantic entrance into your yard or garden, you can't beat this elegant arched gateway with side trellises. It is a project you can tackle and handle easily with common woodworking tools. Get started in mid-winter, about the time the spring seed and bulb catalogs appear in the mailbox. By the time the frost is out of the ground, you'll have your trellis subassemblies constructed and ready for assembly out in the yard.

Build the gateway arches

Building the arches is the most difficult and time-consuming part of this project. You *can* rip thin strips of wood, smear them with glue, and bend them around a form. Known as *glue-lamination bending,* this technique produces a good strong product. But ripping all the strips needed is a lot of work and fairly wasteful of material. We chose to save time and material by *brick-laying* segments to create a blank for each arch, as shown in the drawing on page 59. Two layers of end-laid blocks cut from ⁵⁄₄ × 6 cedar deck boards are glued up in an overlapping sequence, resulting in excellent strength. Cut the arches out from the "bricklaid" blanks once they are glued and dried.

Prepare the blocks for the arch blanks. You'll need stock that's a full inch thick and at least 5 in. wide to make the mitered blocks that are fastened together to form the blanks for the two arches. Because ⁵⁄₄-in.-thick cedar is not readily available in the area where this gateway was built, we used cedar deck boards to make the stock. The nominal ⁵⁄₄ boards are actually

exactly 1 in. thick, so all we needed to do to prepare the stock was to rip-cut the bullnose off each deck board, resulting in 5-in.-wide stock. The majority of the blocks used to make the glue-up blanks are miter-cut at a 72° angle and measure 16 in. along the longer edge. These parts are easy to cut with a power miter saw or radial-arm saw. Simply set the saw to 18° (18° from 90° yields a 72° angle) and cut all 18 of these blocks. We made a stopblock to speed up the process and guarantee uniform parts *(See Photo 1:1).* For the ends of the arches you also need four blocks that are mitered on only one end and measure 8 in. along the longer edge.

Assemble the blanks. In a masonry arch, the *keystone* is the wedge-shaped stone at the crest of the arch that keeps all the other stones in place. In our bricklaid blank, the counterpart to a masonry keystone is the three-part block oriented horizontally at the arch's crest. Begin assembly of this element by drawing setup lines on three blocks for each arch (six blocks total). With a pencil and square, draw a centerline across the width and top edge of each of the blocks. These lines are used to align the blocks during glue-up. The complete glue-up will require around 20 clamps and nearly a pint of water-resistant glue (we used polyurethane glue). Collect your clamps and glue, and pile up the blocks close at hand before you start. Select one of the pieces with the layout marks and spread a nice even coat of glue over the face on one side of the centerline *(See Photo 1:2).* Then, spread glue on a sec-

Photo 1:3 Arrange the two blocks so the centerlines and ends align, then nail the blocks together to hold them in place while you assemble the glue-up. Keep the nails away from the edges so they don't interfere with the saw when cutting out the arches—the nail being driven above did not get in the way, but was a little too close for comfort.

Photo 1:4 Add the third "keystone" block to the assembly and nail it in place. The remaining blocks all "key" off these three, so be sure to get them oriented correctly. Continue adding blocks until the glue-up is completed with the square-cut end blocks. Work quickly so you can get the assembly clamped up before the glue sets.

ond keystone block. Set this second block glued-face to glued-face on the first block, aligning its end with the centerline on the face. Then, align the centerline on the edge of the overlying block with the end of the first keystone block. When everything lines up, nail the blocks together—we used a pneumatic pin nailer *(See Photo 1:3)*, but you can use 6d finishing nails. Position the nails near the center of the overlap so they won't get in the way when cutting the arch contour. Glue the other overlying keystone block to the first block in exactly the same way, butting the ends of the two overlapping blocks together *(See Photo 1:4)*.

Finish gluing up the blanks. You'll need to clamp the glued-up arch blanks together, but wait until the entire unit is glued and nailed together because clamps will keep the assembly from lying flat. When all the blocks are in place, you can go back and apply clamps. So con-

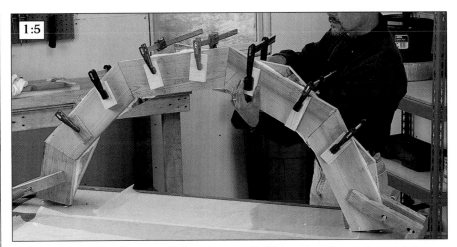

Photo 1:5 Grab any and every clamp you can find lying around your shop and clamp the blocks together. Try to get at least one clamp situated over every block.

tinue along, gluing and driving nails to hold the blocks in place. One layer of the arch is made up of five full blocks (those with two angled ends); the other layer is made up of four full blocks and two of the short blocks with only one angled end. When the first arch is finished, apply clamps around the perimeter of the glue-up *(See*

Photo 1:5). Clamps that can apply pressure a couple of inches in from the edges of the glue-up are best. But as you can see in the photo, we used fast-action bar clamps, some Quick-Grip clamps, and C-clamps, which are ideal for this, along with some handscrews and even some pipe clamps, which are not the best. You need about 20

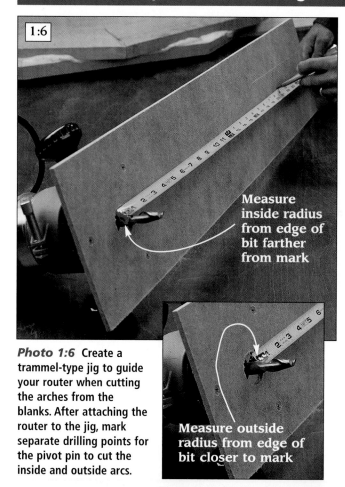

Photo 1:6 Create a trammel-type jig to guide your router when cutting the arches from the blanks. After attaching the router to the jig, mark separate drilling points for the pivot pin to cut the inside and outside arcs.

Measure inside radius from edge of bit farther from mark

Measure outside radius from edge of bit closer to mark

Setting up to cut the arch

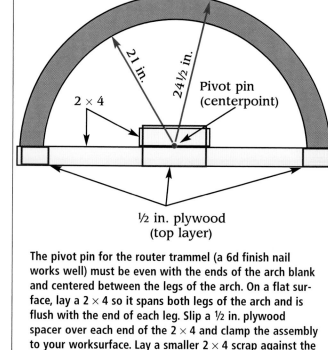

21 in.

24½ in.

2 × 4

Pivot pin (centerpoint)

½ in. plywood (top layer)

The pivot pin for the router trammel (a 6d finish nail works well) must be even with the ends of the arch blank and centered between the legs of the arch. On a flat surface, lay a 2 × 4 so it spans both legs of the arch and is flush with the end of each leg. Slip a ½ in. plywood spacer over each end of the 2 × 4 and clamp the assembly to your worksurface. Lay a smaller 2 × 4 scrap against the top edge of the larger 2 × 4 as a spacer, then attach a piece of ½ in. plywood to the assembly so it covers the seam between 2 × 4s. Drive the pivot pin (nail) into the plywood at the trammel pin centerpoint, then slip each pin hole in the trammel over the nail to cut your arcs.

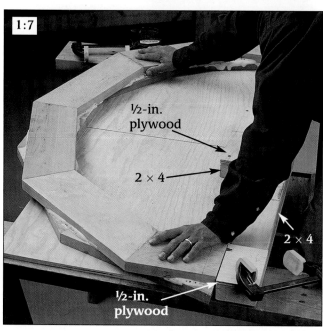

½-in. plywood

2 × 4

2 × 4

½-in. plywood

Photo 1:7 Set up to cut the arches. Secure a blank to a piece of scrap plywood, then secure a 2 × 4 to the worksurface so it spans the feet of the arch. Add ½ in. plywood spacers at the ends of the 2 × 4 and over the midpoint of the 2 × 4, where the pivot pin will be driven (See Illustration, above).

Photo 1:8 With a spiral up-cutting bit in your router, set the trammel jig over the pivot pin in the outside radius location and cut the outside arc. Take several passes, deepening the cut each time. Then, set the inside radius pin hole over the pivot pin and cut the inside arc.

clamps for each assembly. Set the assembly aside and let the glue dry overnight. With all your clamps thus freed, you can glue up the second arch in the same way.

Rout the arches. While the arches could be cut out with a jigsaw or a band saw, your best chance for creating two smooth, even (and identical) arches is to cut them with a router. We used a custom-made hardboard trammel (a pivoting jig used to swing an arc) and a router with a ½-in.-dia. × 2 in. spiral up-cutting bit to cut out the arches. The finished arches are 3½ in. wide. The radius of the outside edges is 24½ in., and the inside edge has a radius of 21 in.

Cut a piece of ¼ in. hardboard to about 12 × 36 in. to make the trammel. Install a spiral up-cutting bit in your router. Measure the distance from the router bit to the edge of the router foot, add a couple of inches, then drill a guide hole slightly larger in diameter than the bit in to the trammel, centered side to side. Remove the base from your router and set it on the trammel so the guide hole is centered on the bit clearance hole in the base. Use the base as a guide for marking the holes for the screws used to attach the base to the router. Drill guide holes at the marks and attach the trammel to the base. Then, measure and mark locations for the guide holes for the trammel pivot pin that will hold the trammel in position while cutting the arc (we used a 6d finish nail for the pivot pin). When measuring back, make sure to mark the drilling points so they align with the guide hole for the bit. The pin hole for cutting the outer radius of the arch should be 24½ in. back from the point where the bit is closest to the pin hole, and the pin hole for cutting the inside radius should be 21 in. back from the point where the bit is farthest from the pin hole *(See Photo 1:6 and inset).* Drill the pin holes with a ⅛-in.-dia. bit.

Secure one of the arch blanks to a flat work surface and set up with 2 × 4 and ½ in. plywood spacers to make the router trim cuts *(See Photo 1:7 and Setting up to cut the arch, previous page).* Adjust the cutting height of the router bit to about ¼ in. Slip the trammel over the pivot pin in the set-up assembly, then make your first cutting pass *(See Photo 1:8).* It doesn't matter if you start with the inside or outside radius, but before cutting, make sure there are no nails in the cutting path of the router bit. Cut all the way through the blank in several passes, lowering the bit about ¼ in. after each pass. Trim both arches in this manner.

Cut mortises in the arches & posts. The arches are joined to the posts with mortise-and-loose-tenon joints. To make these joints, cut mortises in the bottoms of the arches and the tops of the posts, then make a loose tenon to be housed spline-style in opposing mortises. NOTE: *Wait until it's time to install the gate-*

Photo 1:9 **Make a router jig for cutting 1¼ × 2 × 1½-in.-deep mortises into the ends of the posts and the arches. Make a plywood frame to capture the router base and attach it to a small piece of plywood. Base the size of the jig on the distance from the edge of the router bit you'll be using to the edge of your router base (called the setback). In this case, the width of the framed opening should be the setback plus 1¼ in. The length should be the setback plus 2 in. Drill a starter hole for the bit in the middle of the plywood base and rout out the mortise in the base by following the edge guides created by the frame.**

Photo 1:10 **Screw the jig, in turn, to the top of each post to cut mortises for the loose tenons. Each mortise must be centered on the post end. Drill a starter hole into the workpiece then hog out the mortise in multiple passes. We used a 2 in. spiral up-cutting bit to remove the waste.**

way to cut the posts to finished length: uneven ground may require you to vary their height somewhat. To make the mortises, use a router guided by a tenoning jig *(See Photo 1:9).* Attach the jig to a post top with screws and rout out a mortise with the same spiral up-cutting bit used to shape the arches *(See Photo 1:10).* Make the mortises as deep as your bit will allow (preferably, at least 1½ in.). You'll need to make multiple passes to get to full depth: don't try to remove all the waste in one shot. Remove the jig, then use it to rout mortises

Photo 1:11 Use pipe clamps or bar clamps to pin the arches against your workbench, steadying them so you can cut mortises for the loose tenons, as you did with the posts.

Photo 1:13 Lay out the positions for the "rungs" on the arches by measuring out in straight lines, beginning at the peak of the arc. The reference marks for the rungs should be 6⅜ in. apart. Mark each rung by measuring from the previous mark.

Photo 1:14 Attach the rungs to the arches at the marked reference points to create the top of the archway.

Photo 1:12 Cut a piece of stock to 1¼ × 2 in., then round over the edges with a file to match the radius of your router bit. Slice the stock into 3-in. lengths to make the loose tenons.

in the other post and in the ends of the arches *(See Photo 1:11)*. We used pipe clamps to hold the arches and a quick-clamp to hold the post.

Cut some stock to 1¼ × 2 in. to make the tenons that fit into the mortises in the posts and arches. You'll need at least 12 in. of stock. After the stock is cut to size, round over the edges to match the round corners of the mortises, which should equal the radius of your router bit *(See Photo 1:12)*. Then measure the depth of the mortises, multiply by two and subtract ⅛ in. to determine the required length of the tenons. Cut the tenons to length, test the fit to make sure they're snug, then set them aside until you install the gateway in your yard.

Join the arches together. The arches are connected with 11 evenly spaced 1 × 2 "rungs" that follow the curved arch tops. To plot out their positions on the arches, start by making a mark at the very top of one arch, exactly in the center. Using a steel rule, make another mark on the arch where the 6⅜ in. mark on the rule cuts across the arch, measuring from the center mark *(See Photo 1:13)*. Mark the positions for all five rungs on each side of the centerpoint, measuring out 6⅜ in. in straight lines from the previous mark. Transfer the marks onto the other arch, then screw the rungs to the arches, centered on the marks and flush at the ends *(See Photo 1:14).* Use 2½ in. screws (we used stainless steel) to attach the rungs.

Build the trellises

With their elegantly sloping top rails, the trellis wings that flow out on either side of the arch are the most distinctive feature of this gateway project. When combined with the custom trellis frames installed between the archway posts, they also lend the structure a feeling of substance and even romance. Although building the trellis features is somewhat time consuming and requires a table saw, simply compare your final results to the standard lattice sheets you can buy at building centers, and you'll be happy you put forth the effort.

Make the archway trellises. Because they're square, the trellis frames that fit into the sides of the archway are easier to make than the trellis wings, so it's a good idea to build them first and learn the techniques as you go. Each trellis frame holds a gridwork of ½-in.-thick × 1¼-in.-wide lattice strips. The top rails and the stiles for the archway trellises are cut from 2 × 4s, and the bottom rails are cut from 2 × 6s. To make the lattice strips, we planed clear cedar 1 × 6 (¾ × 5½ in.) down to ½ in. thick, then ripped 1¼-in.-wide strips on the table saw. This yielded four 8 ft. strips per board, so we were able to cut lattice for the entire project from nine 8-ft. 1 × 6s.

Rip-cut 2 × 4s to 2½ in. wide for the stiles then cut the stiles and top rails to length (See Cutting List). The ½-in.-wide × 1-in.-deep slots that are cut along the length of the boards capture the ends of the lattice strips. It would be possible to cut these slots using a router and the same jig used to cut the slots in the curbed top rails of the wings trellises, but it's faster and safer to cut them on a table saw. If you have a dado-blade set, you can make the slots in a single pass. Otherwise, set up your saw for a 1-in.-deep cut and run the frame pieces through it in several passes until you've cut ½-in.-wide grooves *(See Photo 2:1).* The inside shoulders of the grooves should start at the centerlines of each board, with the outside shoulders ending up ¼ in. from the faces of the workpieces. The offset grooves allow for the overlap between vertical and horizontal slots (you'll need to pay close attention to the orientation of the offset grooves when cutting the lap joints and assembling the frames).

The joints at the corners of the frames are simple lap joints. Since we used a dado-blade set to cut the slots, we also used it to make the lap cuts. Cut a lap in each end of each frame member *(See Photo 2:2),* removing wood on the faces of the boards containing the slots (this will result in ¾-in.-deep × 3½-in.-wide lap cuts.

Photo 2:1 Cut ½-in.-wide × 1-in.-deep slots in the edge of each square trellis frame rail and stile. We used a table saw and dado-blade set to make these cuts. The slots are offset ¼ in. from the center.

Photo 2:2 Use the dado-blade set to remove waste wood in a hurry, cutting the half-laps at the end of each rail and stile. Pay attention to the orientation of the offset slots.

While not difficult, assembling the trellis units does demand a pretty spacious assembly table. A sheet of plywood laid across a pair of sawhorses is good. The lattice strips don't need to be glued into the framework. A spot of waterproof construction adhesive at each intersection between horizontal and vertical slats may be used to prevent twisting.

Join each bottom rail to two stiles to make a U-shaped frame (don't attach the top rail yet: it should be left off to create access to the slots for installing the lattice strips). Apply glue to the laps and join them together. Check to make sure the joints are square, then reinforce them by nailing or screwing *(See Photo 2:3).*

Install the vertical slats in the frame first. We made a

Photo 2:3
Assemble the bottom rail and stiles of each square trellis frame, using glue and nails. Leave the top rail off so you can insert lattice strips.

2:3

Photo 2:4 Fit the vertical lattice strips into the bottom rail, using a 5¼ in.-wide spacer as a guide. Secure the strips by driving two or three nails through the bottom rail and into each strip.

2:4

Photo 2:5
Install the horizontal lattice strips, starting at the bottom rail. Use the 5¼ in. spacer to set the distance between strips. Pin the strips in place with nails.

2:5

5¼-in.-wide spacer from plywood to help position the slats accurately *(See Photo 2:4)*. Once the slats are positioned, secure them into the bottom rail slot with nails.

When all the vertical strips are locked in place, slide the horizontal strips into the slots in the stiles and distribute them evenly. Use the same spacer to set the positions, beginning at the bottom. Secure both ends of each horizontal lattice strip with nails *(See Photo 2:5)*.

When the latticework is assembled, install the top rail. Apply glue to the lap joints, then slip the top rail in place. Be sure the strips fit into the slot in the rail. Check for square and use the spacer to help hold the positions of the vertical slats at the top of the frame. Drive nail at the lap joints, and into the tops of the slats *(See Photo 2:6)*.

Make the wing trellises. The wing trellises are built in much the same fashion as the square archway trellis units. The difference lies in the gracefully curved top rails on the wings. Because of their contours, making them is a bit more involved than making straight rails. And as a consequence of the rail shape, the lattice slats are not all exactly the same lengths. And you'll need to use a router to cut the slots for the lattice strips, since the table saw can't follow a curve.

Make the stiles and the bottom rails the same way you made them for the archway trellis frames. The only difference is in the lengths of the pieces. The slots and laps are cut the same way.

The top rails for the wing trellis frames are made by creating a template and using it as a guide to rough-cut the shapes from a 2 × 8, then refining the cut by trimming along the template with a router and pattern-following bit.

Draw the rail pattern to scale on a piece of ¼-in.-thick hardboard, using the grid drawing on page 59 as a guide. Cut out the hardboard template with a band saw or a jig saw. With a belt sander or a drum sander chucked in a drill press, sand the edges of the template to smooth out the curves. The ends should form flat, square lines to join neatly to the frame stiles.

Lay the template onto an 8-ft.-long 2 × 8 and trace the pattern of the rail. Trim the extra length from the board, then rough-cut the shape with a jig saw. Cut to within about ⅛ in. of the line *(See Photo 2:7)*. Cut out the rough shapes for both top rails. Next, use double-faced carpet tape to tack the template securely to each rough-cut rail *(See Photo 2:8)*. Install a pattern-following bit in your router (pattern-following bits are flush-cutting bits with a collar at the top of the shank to ride along a template without cutting into it). The workpiece secured, rout around the template with the pattern-following bit set to full cutting depth *(See Photo 2:9)*. The goal here is to create edges on the rail that are as smooth as the template edges. Because the cutting depth of the bit will be less than the thickness of the stock, you'll need to flip the workpiece over, reattach the template to the other side, then shape the rest of the edge.

We used a router with a straight bit and a special jig to cut the slots into the bottom edges of the top rails. Before undertaking this step, note that unlike the slots in the other frame members, the slot in each top rail is a full 1 in. thick because it must accommodate both vertical and horizontal lattice strips. The router "jig" we used is really only two guide blocks that are clamped to the base of the router *(See Photo 2:10)*. A pair of spacers the same width as the workpiece are positioned between the blocks before they're clamped in place. Set the blocks so they are parallel and one is ¼ in. away from the bit (the bit will be offset slightly). Before cutting the slot, drill 1-in.-dia. × 1-in.-deep holes near the ends of rails. Locate the holes so they're centered side to side and the centerpoint is 3½ in. away from the ends of the rails. The holes are starter holes for the router bit you'll use to cut the slots.

Once the starter holes are drilled, the next challenge is to secure the curved rails so they can be routed accurately and safety. We clamped wood screw clamps to each end then clamped the wood screws to sturdy sawhorses. Set a straight router bit to 1 in. cutting depth (if you're using a soft wood like cedar—with harder woods, set a shallower cutting depth and cut the slots in progressively deeper cuts). Set the jig so the block that is ¼ in. away from the bit is on the left side (you'll be pulling the router backwards as you work). Engage the router and cut one side of the slot *(See Photo 2:11)*. When you reach the end of the rail, stop the router and reposition yourself to cut back toward the direction you started from. The block that's

Photo 2:6 Install the top rail after all the strips are in place. Glue and nail the lap joints at the corners, and nail through the rail and into the tops of the lattice strips. Use the spacer to make sure strips don't slip out of alignment during nailing.

Photo 2:7 Use the full-size hardboard template to lay out the shape of the top rail for the trellis wings. Using a jig saw, rough-cut the shape to within about ¹⁄₁₆ in. of the cutting line. Take care not to cut into or past the cutting lines.

Photo 2:8 Use double-faced carpet tape to secure the hardboard template over the rough-cut curved rail.

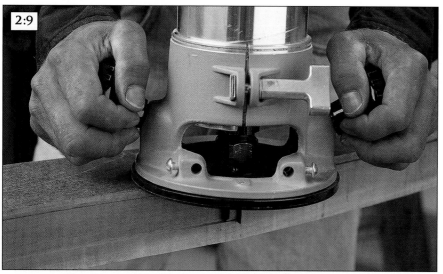

Photo 2:9 Install a pattern-following bit in your router and rout around the rough-cut top rail, smoothing out the shape as you follow the template. After routing all the way around, remove the template and tape it to the other face of the workpiece. Rout the edge from this side to finish the smoothing cut.

Photo 2:10
Clamp wood blocks to your router base to set up the router for slot-cutting the curved rail. Use cut-off pieces of the rail material to set the distance between blocks. Secure the blocks so the bit is offset (the edge should be ¼ in. away from one block).

¼ in. away from the bit should be on the other side of the workpiece. Start the router and cut the other side of the slot *(See Photo 2:12)*. The router base should contact as much of the workpiece as possible as you rout. If the router begins to bog down, stop the cut and raise the bit so you're removing less stock, then cut the slot in multiple passes. Cut slots in both top rails.

Cut half-laps in the ends of the wing trellis top rails to mate with the half-laps in the tops of the stiles. Once again, the curves of the rails make it difficult to perform this operation on a table saw. We simply laid out the half-laps, then used a circular saw to remove strips of wood to the correct depth in the waste area *(See Photo 2:13)*. Then we removed the strips of left-over wood and smoothed the joint with a chisel *(See Photo 2:14)*.

Join the bottoms rails and stiles (but not the top rails) with glue and nails, making sure the lap joints are square. Dry-fit the top rail into position. Cut the vertical lattice strips so they're each a couple of inches longer than their finished length. Dry-fit the strips in the bottom rail slots of one wing, using the 5¼ in. spacer as a guide. The lattice strips should overlay the top rail. The top ends will need to be trimmed to follow the curve of the top rail. At the high point of each intersection between the top rail and the strips, measure up 1 in. and mark each strip. *(See Photo 2:15)*. Then, use a straightedge to extend the mark toward the lower point of intersection, following the line of the top rail *(See Photo 2:16)*. Remove the lattice strips and trim them to length.

Replace the strips in the bottom rail and dry-fit the top rail over the free ends. Check to make sure none of the strips is too long. Nail the bottom ends in place. Four of the horizontal lattice strips on each trellis are square cut to fit between

Photo 2:11 Drill a starter hole for your router bit, then fit the router with guide blocks over the curved edge of the rail. Rout out one side of the slot area.

Photo 2:12 Rout back along the opposite face of the workpiece, this time with the positions of the guide blocks reversed. The resulting slot you cut should be ¼ in. from each edge of the workpiece.

Photo 2:13 Use a circular saw to cut out the waste wood to make the half-laps at the ends of the curved top rail. Cut ¾-in.-deep saw kerfs from the end of the board to the lap shoulder.

Photo 2:14 Clean up and smooth the half-lap joints with a sharp wood chisel.

the stiles. Position them in the stile slots, using the spacer for reference. The top three horizontal strips on each trellis need to be contoured on the end that intersects the top rail (the contoured end is fitted into the slot in the top rail). Dry-lay them in position and mark the contours as you did for the vertical rails. Cut them to fit, then nail the horizontal strips in place, starting at the bottom *(See Photo 2:17)*. Install the lattice strips on both trellises.

Join the top rails to the stiles with glue and nails. You'll notice that there are ½ in. gaps between some of the lattice strips and the shoulders of the slots. These gaps need to be filled with filler blocks. Use cut-off pieces of lattice strip to make the blocks, trimming them so they'll be flush with the bottom edge of the top rail. Set the blocks into the gaps, then secure them with glue and nails *(See Photo 2:18)*. If you're using a hammer and finish nails, not a pneumatic nailer, drill pilot holes first. Now, cut filler blocks to fit between the ends of all the slats in all bottom rails and attach them with glue and nails *(See Photo 2:19)*.

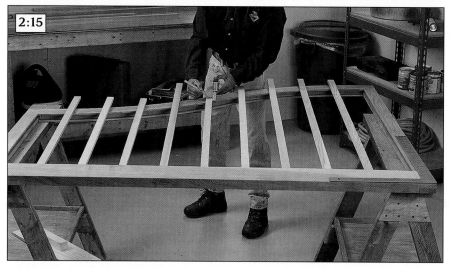

Photo 2:15 Join the bottom rail and the stiles for each wing frame with glue and nails. Dry-fit vertical lattice strips in the bottom slot. To mark the strips for trimming, start by measuring up 1 in. from the high side where each strip crosses the top rail.

Photo 2:16 Extend cutting lines across the top of each vertical lattice strip by following a straightedge that's roughly parallel to the curve of the frame.

Photo 2:17 After the vertical strips are cut to fit, pin them into the bottom rails. Then begin installing the horizontal strips, starting at the bottom. Use the spacer and fasten the strips at the stiles as you work.

Photo 2:18 When all the vertical and horizontal strips are fitted into the top rails, glue and nail the lap joints, then cut spacers to fill the gaps between strips and the top rail slots (there will be a ½-in. gap on one side of each strip). Use cutoff pieces of lattice to make the spacers. Secure them with glue and nails.

Photo 2:19 Fill the gaps between lattice strip ends in all bottom rails of each trellis frame, and secure the fillers with glue and nails. NOTE: If you're using a hammer and nails, not a nail gun, it's a good idea to drill pilot hole for the nails first. You can do this easily by chucking one of the finish nails you're using into your drill and using it as a drill bit.

Photo 3:1 Lay out the location for the gateway using batter-boards and mason's strings.

Photo 3:3 Drive stakes and use a mason's string so you can check to make sure the post anchors are all aligned with one another. Measure from the bottom of the post-anchor saddle to determine the required height of each post.

Photo 3:2 We used one-piece stake-and-post-anchor hardware to secure the posts, rather than messing with pouring footings. Drive the stakes at the post locations, doing your best to get them level and aligned correctly. A chunk of 4 × 4 placed in the saddle portion absorbs the blows from the maul.

Photo 3:4 Trim the posts to the correct height with a circular saw. It's likely the heights will all be a little different to account for uneven terrain.

Assemble & install the gateway

The gateway is not designed to be freestanding. One way to anchor it to the ground is to pour concrete footings and attach the posts to the footings with metal post anchors (See page 30). But if you'd rather not go to all that effort, use stake-and-post-anchor hardware. These anchors are equipped with an integral, two-sided metal stake that you simply drive into the ground at the post locations. Then you fit the post into the saddle portion of the device and tighten the nuts and bolts to cinch the saddle around the post.

Lay out the site & install the archway. Use batter-boards and mason's string to lay out the post locations for the gateway (See pages 27 to 28 Gazebo).You should have strings intersecting at each post location. Make sure to level the strings *(See Photo 3:1)*. Drive the stake-and-post anchors at each post location. Before driving them, cut a scrap of 4 × 4 about 6 in. long and place it in the saddle to absorb the shock of the sledge or maul. Drive the stake about halfway in, then stop and check to make sure it is going in straight, using a level *(See Photo 3:2)*. Adjust as needed, then finish driv-

Photo 3:5 Attach the archway (square) trellises to the archway posts by driving 3-in. deck screws through the trellis frame stiles and into the posts.

ing the hardware home. Drive all the stake/anchors so the bottoms of the saddles are at grade. Any compensation for uneven ground will be made by adjusting the heights of the posts when they're trimmed.

Drive stakes at the ends of the main run of four posts and connect them with a line level. Set the line at the highest anchor and measure the distance from the bottom of each post saddle to the line (See Photo 3:3). Also check the height of the two archway post anchors. The highest anchor (the one closest to the level line) should be fitted with a 66¾-in.-long post. For the other posts (if different) add the distance further from the line than the high post to 66¾ in., and cut to that length with a circular saw (See Photo 3:4). Be sure you don't trim off an end with a mortise cut for a loose tenon.

Attach the square archway trellises to the posts that form the four corners of the archway. The tops of the trellis frames should be the same distance (2 in.) down from the post tops. To attach the frames, lay the posts on their sides on a worksurface, making sure the mortised post ends are at the same end (the top). Position a few ⅞-in. spacers next to each post to support the frame and raise it to the correct position. Drill pilot holes, then drive 3½ in. screws through the slots in the frame stiles and into the posts (See Photo 3:5). Drive a screw every foot or so. Join the frames and posts into two assemblies that form the "walls" of the archway.

Set one of the assemblies into the post

Photo 3:6 Set the archway post-and-trellis assemblies into the saddle of the post anchors and tighten the bolts to hold them in place (inset photo).

anchors and press it down to make sure it's well seated. Tighten the bolts on the post anchors so the saddles fit snugly around the bottoms of the posts. The assembly should be freestanding at this point. Install the assembly on the other side of the archway and tighten the saddle bolts *(See Photo 3:6 and inset).*

Set a loose tenon in each post-top mortise in the archway. You may need to rap the tenons lightly to seat them—if you find you need a hammer or mallet to drive them in, they're too big and should be sanded down a bit. Once again with a helper, raise the top of the archway so it rests on top of the posts. Carefully position the top so the mortises in the bottoms of the arches line up over the free ends of the loose tenons *(See Photo 3:7).* Pull down carefully on the top, if necessary, until the posts and the arches butt together flush. To pin the top in place, drive a pair of 6d finish nails into each tenon: one nail through the post and the other through the arch.

Attach the end posts to the short ends of the wing trellises the same way you attached the taller posts to the archway frames *(See Photo 3:8).* Set the short posts into their anchors and tighten the bolts until snug. Loosely clamp the free end of each wing to the shared archway post. Adjust the wing trellis frame until it is centered on the shared post and perpendicular to the archway frame. The bottom rails should all align. Tighten the clamps so the wings don't slip out of position, then attach them to the shared posts with 3½ in. screws driven through pilot holes in the frame stiles *(See Photo 3:9).* This essentially completes the installation of the primary gateway parts. Check to make sure everything is square, then cinch up the post anchor bolts so they're good and tight (but do not overtighten them).

Photo 3:7 Fit a loose tenon into each post-top mortise. With a helper, lower the archway top into position. Press down on the archway, if needed, until the tenons are fully seated in the archway mortises. Don't glue the tenons; but it's a good idea to drive a 6d nail through both the post and archway to pin the tenons in place at each joint.

Photo 3:8 Attach the wing trellis frames to the outer posts with 3-in. deck screws.

Photo 3:9
Set the wing trellises into the appropriate post saddles and adjust their positions until they're level, plumb and at a right angle to the archway trellis frames. Join the wings to the shared post with 3½-in. deck screws.

Photo 3:10
Cut filler strips to fill the gaps between the arches and the posts, then miter-cut 1 × 2 trim to conceal the joint. Attach the trim pieces with stainless steel finish nails.

Photo 3:11 Cut and attach a flat post cap to each post, then conceal the cap joint with more mitered 1 × 2 trim.

Photo 3:12 Apply your finish of choice. We used clear wood sealer.

Finishing touches. The transition molding overlaps the top edges of the post. It punctuates the jump from the 4 × 4 post to the smaller-sectioned arch, and it offers a vehicle for sealing the top of the post.

The legs of the arches will be recessed about ¾ to ⅞ in. per side from the parallel faces of the posts in the archway. Measure the exact size of these gaps and cut ¾-in.-high filler strips to fit. The outer faces and ends of the strips should be flush with the posts. Attach the filler strips to the post arches with construction adhesive.

Rip-cut ½- × 1½-in. strips of molding to apply over the joints between the posts and arches. Miter-cut the ends to wrap around the posts. Attach the mitered molding with 6d finish nails (See Photo 3:10). The tops of the molding strips should be flush with the tops of the filler strips. When the molding is installed, apply clear caulk to the seams between the pieces on the post top. This will retard water penetration.

Cut 3½-in.-square pieces of ¾-in. cedar to cap the short posts on the ends of the gateway wings. The post caps help prevent water from wicking into the exposed end grain at the post tops. Attach them with construction adhesive and 6d finish nails. Knock the cap edges back with a file or sander if they project out past the faces of the posts.

Cut ½- × 1½-in. strips of wood to frame the tops of the short posts, concealing the seams between the post caps and the posts. Miter the ends and install as with the frames around the arch/post joints (See Photo 3:11).

Set any exposed nailheads with a nailset and sand down any rough areas on the gateway. Wipe clean, then apply your finish of choice. We applied clear wood sealer to protect the wood.

LANDSCAPE BRIDGE

Graceful and engaging, a landscape bridge can brighten backyards or gardens even in the flattest and driest surroundings. Add a little romance to your living spaces (and have some fun in the shop) by building this "portable" bridge yourself.

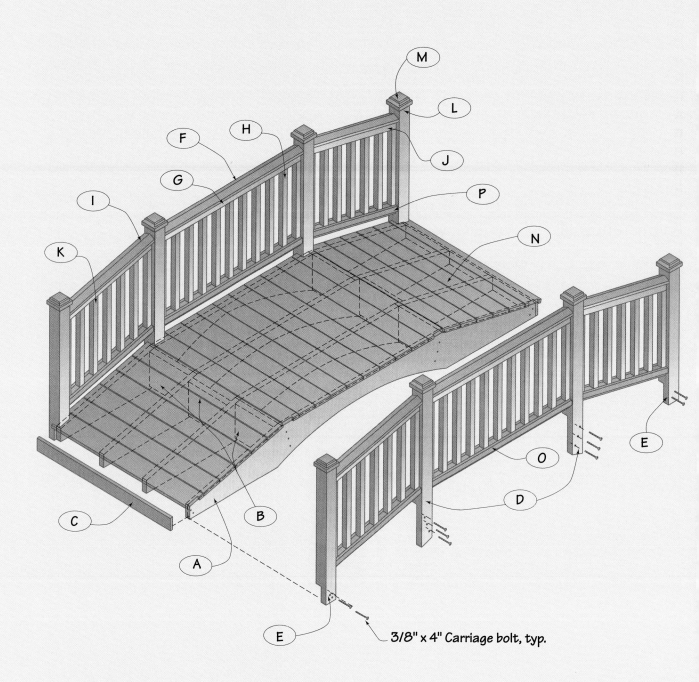

3/8" x 4" Carriage bolt, typ.

OVERALL DIMENSIONS ($51 \times 122^{1}/_{2} \times 47^{3}/_{4}$")

KEY	PART NAME	QTY.	SIZE	MATERIAL
MAIN STRUCTURE				
A	JOIST	4	$1^{1}/_{2} \times 11^{1}/_{4} \times 120$"	PRESSURE TREATED
B	BLOCKING	6	$1^{1}/_{2} \times 10^{3}/_{8} \times 13^{1}/_{2}$"	PRESSURE TREATED
C	FASCIA	2	$^{3}/_{4} \times 3^{3}/_{4} \times 46^{1}/_{2}$"	CEDAR
D	RAIL POST	4	$3^{1}/_{2} \times 3^{1}/_{2} \times 45^{1}/_{4}$"	CEDAR
E	RAIL POST	4	$3^{1}/_{2} \times 3^{1}/_{2} \times 39$"	CEDAR
F	HANDRAIL	2	$1^{1}/_{2} \times 3^{1}/_{2} \times 48^{1}/_{2}$"	CEDAR
G	BALUSTER RAIL	4	$1^{1}/_{2} \times 2^{1}/_{2} \times 48^{1}/_{2}$"	CEDAR
H	BALUSTER	22	$1^{1}/_{2} \times 1^{1}/_{2} \times 23^{1}/_{4}$"	CEDAR
I	RAMPED HANDRAIL	4	$1^{1}/_{2} \times 3^{1}/_{2} \times 31$"**	CEDAR
J	RAMPED BALUSTER RAIL	8	$1^{1}/_{2} \times 2^{1}/_{2} \times 31$"**	CEDAR
K	RAMPED BALUSTER	28	$1^{1}/_{2} \times 1^{1}/_{2} \times 24^{3}/_{8}$"	CEDAR
L	POST BRIM	8	$1 \times 4^{1}/_{2} \times 4^{1}/_{2}$"	CEDAR
M	POST CAP	8	$1 \times 3^{1}/_{2} \times 3^{1}/_{2}$"	CEDAR
N	DECKING	22	$1 \times 5^{1}/_{2} \times 47^{1}/_{2}$"	CEDAR
O	RAIL CLADDING	4	$^{3}/_{4} \times 1^{1}/_{2} \times 48^{1}/_{2}$"	CEDAR
P	RAMPED RAIL CLADDING	8	$^{3}/_{4} \times 1^{1}/_{2} \times 31$"	CEDAR

** INDICATES CUT TO FIT

HARDWARE REQUIRED

DECK SCREWS			$\#8 \times 3$", $2^{1}/_{2}$"	
CARRIAGE BOLTS		20	$^{3}/_{8} \times 4$"	W/NUTS & WASHERS

> **NOTICE: Part dimensions are based on ideal installation conditions. For best results, confirm measurements on actual project before cutting parts.**

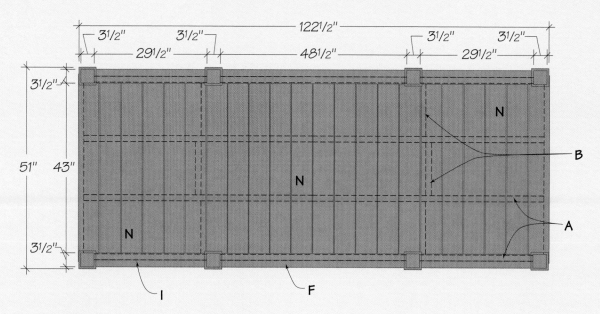

PLAN VIEW

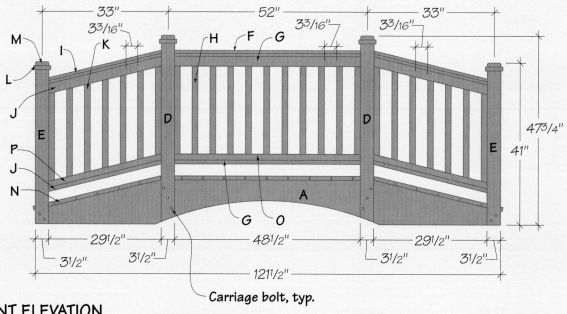

Carriage bolt, typ.

FRONT ELEVATION

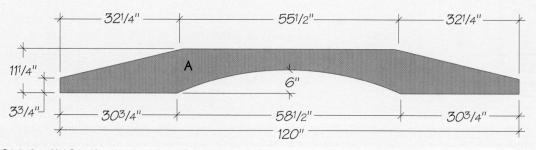

JOIST LAYOUT

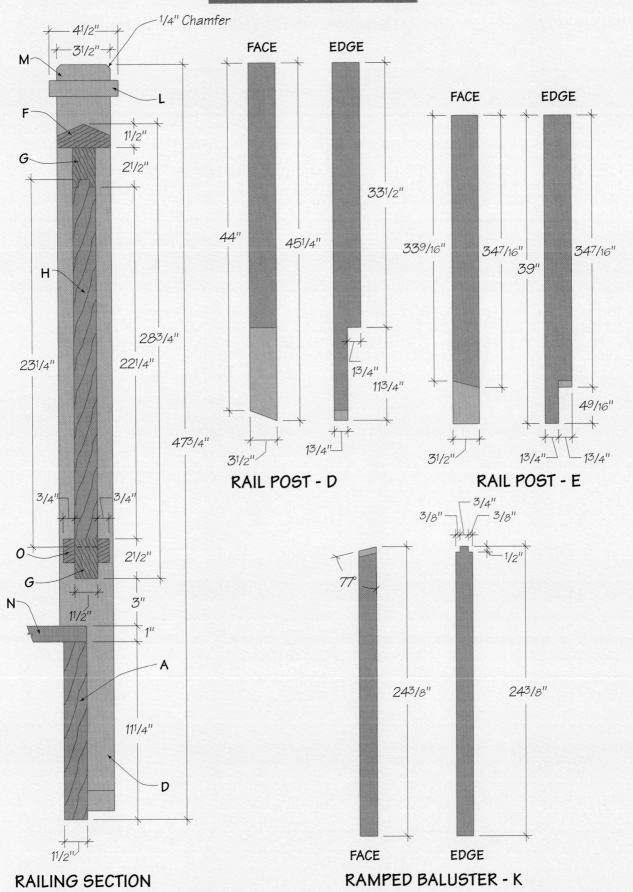

4¹/₂"
3¹/₂"
¹/₄" Chamfer
M
L
F
G
H
23¹/₄"
22¹/₄"
28³/₄"
47³/₄"
1¹/₂"
2¹/₂"
³/₄"
³/₄"
O
G
2¹/₂"
N
3"
1¹/₂"
1"
A
11¹/₄"
D
1¹/₂"

RAILING SECTION

FACE   EDGE

44"
45¹/₄"
33¹/₂"
1³/₄"
11³/₄"
3¹/₂"
1³/₄"

RAIL POST - D

FACE   EDGE

33⁹/₁₆"
34⁷/₁₆"
34⁷/₁₆"
39"
49/₁₆"
3¹/₂"
1³/₄"
1³/₄"

RAIL POST - E

³/₄"
³/₈"
³/₈"
¹/₂"
77°
24³/₈"
24³/₈"

FACE   EDGE

RAMPED BALUSTER - K

Photos by Apple River Studios

Photo 1 Use a 1-in.-wide strip of ¼-in.-thick hardboard to flex an arc for laying out the arches at the bottoms of the joists.

Photo 2 Cut the tapers at the ends of the joists with a circular saw and straightedge. The tapers create the "rise" in the bridge.

Photo 3 Stagger the blocking that fits between joists to create access for attaching the blocking boards to the joists. The tops of the blocking must be beveled to match the slope of the tapered joists.

Photo 4 Attach fascia boards to the ends of the joists at each end of the bridge. The fascia also must be beveled to follow the slope line of the joists.

Function and beauty combine in this appealing landscape bridge. In addition to providing a lovely landscape feature to look at, it's wide enough and sturdy enough to allow you to push a lawn mower or small wheelbarrow across. The obvious use of a bridge like this is to span a small stream: It's especially useful if the stream divides your property, making access to the far side difficult. But even without a body of water to cross, a bridge can enhance and beautify your yard. Use it to span a hollow, swale or rocky outcropping. Or create the illusion of a stream by spreading landscaping stones in a meandering path beneath the bridge.

Reduced to its essentials, the bridge consists of four joists joined with blocking, posts, deck boards and a railing on each side. As shown, the bridge is about 12 feet long and four feet wide, but you can scale it to suit your needs and the appearance you want for your yard

(but try to maintain a walkway that's at least 32 in. wide). This landscape bridge is a carpentry project that's best built in your shop, then moved to the site for assembly, installation and finishing.

Build the joist framework

The landscape bridge is supported by four arched and tapered joists connected with 2 × 12 blocking. A beveled fascia board is attached to each set of joist ends to cap the ends of the bridge. The four joists are cut from 10-ft.-long 2 × 12s. Lay out and cut one joist then use it as a template for making the other three.

The arcs at the bottom edges of the joists can be laid out by flexing a 1-in.-wide strip of ¼ in. hardboard between the end points of the arc. Mark the end points along the bottom edge, 30¾ in. from each end. Then, find the midpoint of the 2 × 12 (60 in.), measure up 6 in. and drive a small nail. Clamp the hardboard strip to the workpiece so the ends fall across the endpoint marks and the peak of the strip is pressed against the nail. Trace the arc onto the board *(See Photo 1)*. Remove the strip and cut out the arc with a jig saw. Sand the edge of the cut smooth.

Taper the ends of the joist: First, measure up 3¾ in. from the bottom edge on each end of the joist and make a reference mark. Then, measure 31⅜ in. along the top edge from the top corner above each reference mark. Connect the marks at each end to make cutting lines. Make the taper cuts with a jig saw or circular saw and a straight-edge *(See Photo 2)*. Lay out and cut the rest of the joists.

The joists are connected with pieces of blocking cut to 13½ in. long and 10⅜ in. wide from 2 × 12 stock. Fascia boards beveled on the top edges are nailed to the ends of the joists. Because of the angle of the tapers cut on the joists, the blocking will need to be trimmed a bit. You can plane the blocking flush with the top edges of the joists after it is installed with a hand plane or hand-held power plane. Otherwise, hold them in place between the joists and mark the amount of stock that needs to be trimmed away. Bevel-cut to the lines with a circular saw, jigsaw or table saw.

The blocking should be aligned with the "break" on the top edges of the joists (where the taper levels off). But to allow you to screw through the joists and into the ends of each piece of blocking, stagger the blocking.

Working on a flat surface, line the pieces of blocking up so the tops are flush with the tops of the joists and install them by end-screwing through the joists and into the blocking. Drive three #8 × 3 in. deck screws per joint *(See Photo 3)*.

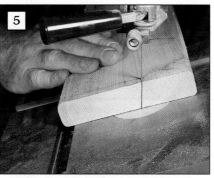

Photo 5 Notch the ends of the deck boards to fit around the posts. The notches in the deck boards need to be cut at an angle to fit against the posts.

Photo 7 Clamp each post to the joist framework and adjust it so it's level and plumb before you attach it. The deck board shown is dry-fit as a spacer.

The top edges of the fascia boards are beveled at a 13° angle. Cross-cut the boards to length, then rip the bevel on a table saw or with your circular saw. Attach the fascia boards to the ends of the joists *(See Photo 4)*.

Install the posts

The posts are cut with half-laps to make lap joints where they fit against the joist framework. The deck boards that intersect with the posts are notched to fit. The surest way to lay out the half-laps for the end posts is to notch and dry-install the end deck boards, then cut the posts to fit over them. To mark the end deck boards for notching, first mark the inside edge of each post on the outer joists. The posts should be flush with the ends of the joist framework, so

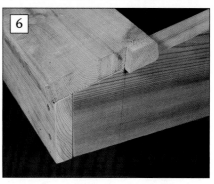

Photo 6 The deck boards at the ends of the bridge are flush with the outer joists in the notched area and overhang the joists and fascia by ½ in. elsewhere.

Photo 8 Drill counterbored guide holes for the carriage bolts that secure the posts. Drive bolts into the guide holes and secure with washers and nuts.

measure in 3½ in. from each end. Then, lay the deck board across the joists so it overhangs the fascia by ½ in. Extend the line for the post edges up onto each end of the deck board. Measure in ½ in. at the top of the cutting line and draw a cutting line parallel to the end of the board. With a band saw, jig saw or hand saw, make the ½-in.-deep cut at the edge of the notch, following the cutting angle *(See Photo 5)*. Remove the wood from the notched area by making the long cut parallel to the board end. Notch both ends. Test the fit of the deck board *(See Photo 6)* then screw it temporarily in place (you'll want to remove it before installing the posts so you can get better access to the fasteners). Notch and install both end boards.

Cut the end posts to length, then

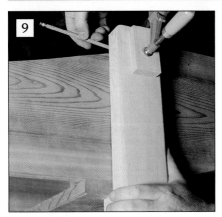

Photo 9 Trace the joist arch profile onto the bottom of each post.

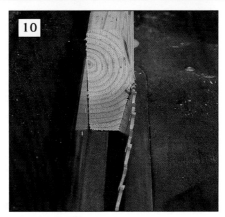

Photo 10 Chamfer the top of the hand rail stock at 15° from both directions.

cut half-lap joints in the posts so they fit over the end deck boards and are flush with the bottoms of the joists. The easiest way to cut the half-laps is to use a dado-blade set installed in your table saw (See *Cutting half-laps,* right). Keep in mind that the shoulders of the half-laps in the end posts must slope to follow the tapers at the ends of the joists. To cut them, you'll need to set the table saw miter gauge to a 13° angle when making the initial pass or two at the top of the half-lap notch. Cut the first half-lap, then position the post and clamp it in place *(See Photo 7).* Check with a level and framing square to make sure the post is vertical

and plumb. Cut all four end posts, checking to make sure they fit correctly, then attach them to the joists with two ⅜ × 4 in. carriage

Cutting half-laps

Notching a post to create a half-lap for a lap joint is easy to do with a table saw and dado-blade set. When notching large stock, like the 4 × 4 post at right, you'll need to make at least two passes of increasing depth to keep the blades from bogging down. Using a miter gauge as a guide, feed the workpiece through the blades in the outlined area (Photo 1), leaving a narrow nub of uncut material for the workpiece to ride on. Make another pass to full depth, then knock off the nub with a hammer (Photo 2). Flatten the shoulder and cheek of the notch with a chisel (Photo 3).

bolts at each end post, driven into counterbored guide holes. Drill the counterbore and guide holes, then drive the carriage bolts through the guide holes with a hammer *(See Photo 8).* Secure the carriage bolts with washers and ⅜-in. nuts.

Install the higher midposts. Unlike the end posts, these posts have square half-laps, which makes them easier to cut. Simply cut the posts slightly overlong, then cut a half-lap at the bottom of each post. Set a deck board on the joists as a spacer. Clamp each post in place, then trace the arc of the outer joist onto the bottom end of the post *(See Photo 9).* Cut the arc shape with a jig saw then attach the posts with carriage bolts, as with the end posts. Remove the deck board spacers.

Build & install the railings

The deck railings are formed by capturing 2 × 2 balusters between top and bottom rails, then capping the top rail with a wide handrail. Each rail is made in three sections to fit between the posts. The balusters have tenon-style tongues on top to fit into grooves that run the length of each top rail. At the bottom, the balusters are left full size and fit into dadoes cut across the bottom rail. To hide the bottom rail/baluster joints, 1× 2 cladding is attached to the outer faces of the bottom rails. Double-check all Cutting List measurements against the actual distances between your posts before cutting the parts for the railings—it's reasonable to expect to find some variation.

The baluster rails are cut from 2 × 3 stock (you'll probably need to rip-cut 2 × 4s to width), and the handrails are fashioned from 2 × 4s. The handrails are chamfered on top to shed water and make them more comfortable to hold. Although you won't be cutting the handrails to fit until the railing is installed, go ahead and cut the chamfers now. When the chamfers are cut, the handrails will slope from 1½ in. thick at the middles to ¾ in. thick at the edges. To produce these chamfers, you need to make two bevel-rip cuts. While the chamfers can be cut with a circular saw, the best tool for this job is the table saw. Raise the blade and tilt it to 15°. Set the fence so it's ¾ in. away from the point where the blade will meet the stock, then cut the first chamfer. Turn the workpiece over and make the second bevel cut to complete the chamfer *(See Photo 10).*

Miter-cut the ends of the short handrail sections at 13° angles. Be sure the cuts on the ends of each handrail section are parallel. Sand the handrails thoroughly and set them aside.

The balusters are joined to the top rails with tongue-and-groove joints. Cut the groove (¾ in. wide × ½ in. deep) in the bottom edge of the rail. This can be done with a router and ¾-in. straight bit, using edge guides. But we used the table saw and dado-blade set. Cut grooves in all top rails *(See Photo 11).*

Before making the bottom baluster rails, make the balusters so you can use them to guide your work. Begin the process by ripping and cross-cutting stock to the dimensions specified by the Cutting List. The balusters for the level section of railing are square-cut, but those for the angled railing sections are mitered at 13° on the top ends to follow the slope of the handrail (which follows the slope of the joist tapers). Cut the tongues at the ends of each baluster by setting up your dado-blade set to make a ⅜-in.-deep × ½-in.-wide rabbet cut, then run all four faces of each baluster end through the blade (this will create tongues that are ¾ in. thick and ½ in. deep). Attach an auxiliary fence to your miter gauge to guide the workpieces. Also attach a reference block to your rip fence to align your workpieces—the reference block should be ½ in. outside the point where the blades contact the workpiece *(See Photo 12).* To cut the tongues on the mitered balusters, simply adjust the miter gauge so the end of each baluster butts flat against the reference block.

The bottom rails are cut with a series of dadoes to accommodate the bottom ends of the balusters. Start by laying out the dadoes on the straight rails that fit on the flat portion of the bridge. TIP: *Cut the rails for each side of the bridge to length then lay them next to one another edge-to-edge so you can lay out baluster locations on both rails at the same time.* Outline baluster locations at each end, then mark the midpoint of the rail and center a baluster at that point. Lay out field balusters from the middle to the ends on each side. There are 11 balusters in total, so the spacing should be about 3³⁄₁₆ in. between balusters. Depending on the actual size of your stock, you may need to play with the spacing a bit, though. This is why it helps to have

Photo 11 Cut a ¾-in.-wide × ½-in.-deep groove in the bottom of each top rail to hold the baluster tongues.

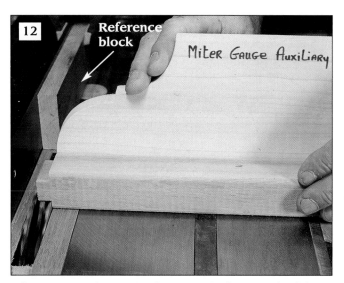

Photo 12 Cut the tenon-style tongues in the top ends of the baluster by running each face through the dado-blade set.

all the balusters cut so you physically lay them on the rails for reference. To avoid confusion as you are cutting, shade the waste areas with a pencil. Set up the dado cutter at its maximum cutting width and adjust the depth of cut to ½ in. Move the rip fence out of the way; you'll use the miter gauge to guide the rails across the cutter. Run the rails over the dado head to remove the wood in the dado locations. Again, you can save some time by ganging the rails together.

The setup is slightly different for cutting the dadoes in the angled rails that fit into the ramped sections of the bridge. For these, the dado set must be tilted at a 13° angle. Plus, you'll need to make two passes for each dado, with the blades set at different heights to create a smooth-bottomed dado with the correct pitch. The first, shallower, cut should be ¼ in. deep at the lower side. The shallower bite of the second cut should be the same depth as the higher side of the first cut.

Photo 13 Set the cutting angle of the dado-blade set to 13° and cut dadoes in the bottom rail to hold the balusters in the ramped railing sections. The low end of the second pass should be the same height as the high end of the first pass.

Photo 14 Secure the balusters in the bottom-rail dadoes with glue (we used polyurethane glue) and one 3-in. deck screw driven into each baluster. When using polyurethane glue, moisten the wood slightly before applying the glue.

This gets a little tricky, so it's a good idea to practice a few cuts on some 2 × 2 scrap first. And be sure to lay out the baluster positions carefully, as you did for the rails for the flat portion. Cut all the dadoes for these four rails *(See Photo 13)*.

Assemble the railing sections using glue and 3-in.-long deck screws. Lay out all the parts for a section on a flat surface. To begin, apply glue to the baluster dadoes in the bottom rail. Use a disposable brush to spread the glue evenly. Apply glue to the tongues on the baluster tops, too. Fit the top railing groove over the baluster tongues and fit the bottoms of the balusters into the corresponding dadoes in the bottom rail. Drill a pilot hole and drive one deck screw through the bottom of the bottom rail and into each baluster end *(See Photo 14)*. Check with a framing square or by measuring the diagonals to make sure the section is square, and adjust as needed. Then, drive screws through the top rail and into the baluster tops. It's not a bad idea to clamp the section in two directions while the glue sets to keep it from falling out of square. Assemble all railing sections in this manner.

Install the decking & apply the finish

The decking adds greatly to the weight of the bridge structure. Because it is not time consuming to install, consider cutting the boards to fit in your shop, then moving them to the installation site.

Install the deck boards you've already cut and notched to fit around the posts by sliding them under the posts, then driving a pair of 3 in. deck screws through the boards and into each joist. The end boards should overhang the fascia by ½ in. All deck boards that do not butt up against a post should overhang the outer joists by ½ in. Lay the deck boards across the joists, using 16d common nails as spacers between boards. If the deck board layout doesn't come out

exactly right, make adjustments of less than 1 in. total by ripping one board (the last board before the flat area of the walkway is a good choice). If you need to remove more than 1 in., spread it out over two or more deck boards to preserve some uniformity. When building the bridge, we did not need to make any adjustments to the deck board widths. The screw heads should be countersunk.

Once the decking is installed, go ahead and install the railing sections. Set 3 in. spacers at each end of the opening, set the railing section onto the spacers and attach it to the posts at each end with deck screws. Then, measure the distances between posts and cut the pieces of the chamfered handrail to fit (you'll need to miter-cut the ends of the shorter sections). Attach the handrail with construction adhesive and a few screws driven up through the top rail and into the hand rail in each section. To conceal the dadoes and baluster bottoms, rip-cut some 1× stock to 1½ in. wide, then cut pieces to clad both sides of the bottom rails. Round over the edges then attach the cladding with 6d stainless steel finishing nails.

Cap the posts. The caps have two parts, a square cap made of ⁵⁄₄ deck boards, which overhang the post by ½ in. all around, and a smaller, chamfered cap that is centered on top of the square cap. Cut the parts to the dimensions specified by the Cutting List. The chamfers on the smaller cap are formed by trimming with a chamfering bit in a router table, or by hand-filing. Once the pieces are cut, installation is a matter of aligning them on the post and fastening them. The lower cap piece can be attached with two or three screws driven at slight angles into the post top. The "cap" is nailed to the brim with finish nails.

Finally, apply a coat of stain or water sealer to the bridge, if desired.

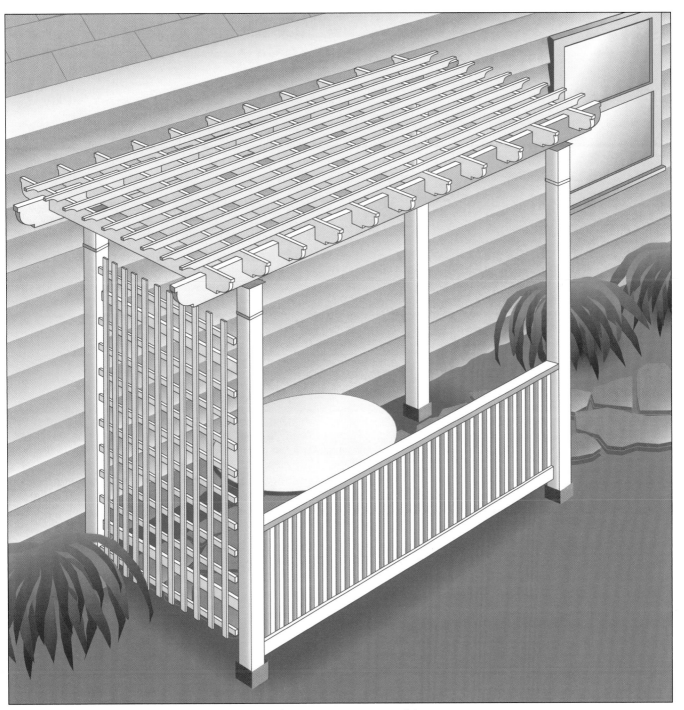

Arbor/Trellis

An arbor is an open, overhead structure supported by posts and typically used to train plants and to provide shade. A trellis is a vertical matrix of slats or lathe that can also be used to train plants, while creating an exterior "room divider." When combined, these structures form an Arbor/Trellis that adds tranquility and privacy to your yard.

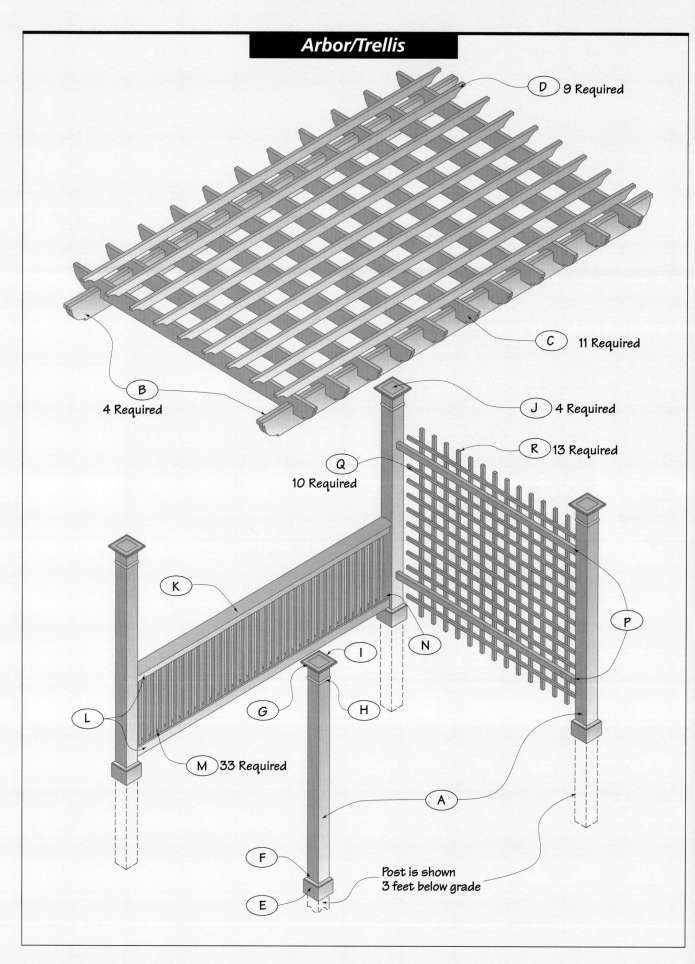

D 9 Required

C 11 Required

B
4 Required

J 4 Required

R 13 Required

Q
10 Required

K

P

N

I

G H

L

M 33 Required

A

F

E

Post is shown
3 feet below grade

OVERALL DIMENSIONS (120 × 192 × 112$\frac{1}{2}$")

KEY	PART NAME	QTY.	SIZE	MATERIAL
MAIN STRUCTURE				
A	POST	4	5$\frac{1}{2}$ × 5$\frac{1}{2}$ × 131"	EXTERIOR LUMBER
B	BEAM	4	1$\frac{1}{2}$ × 9$\frac{1}{4}$ × 192"	EXTERIOR LUMBER
C	RAFTER	11	1$\frac{1}{2}$ × 7$\frac{1}{4}$ × 120"	EXTERIOR LUMBER
D	PURLIN	9	1$\frac{1}{2}$ × 3$\frac{1}{2}$ × 176$\frac{1}{2}$"	EXTERIOR LUMBER
E	BASEBOARD	16	1 × 5$\frac{1}{2}$ × 7$\frac{1}{2}$"	EXTERIOR LUMBER
F	QUARTER-ROUND MOLDING	16	$\frac{3}{4}$ × 3/4 × 7"	PINE
G	COVE MOLDING	16	$\frac{5}{8}$ × 2$\frac{3}{4}$ × 9$\frac{1}{4}$"	PINE
H	HALF-ROUND MOLDING	16	$\frac{1}{2}$ × 1 × 6$\frac{1}{2}$"	PINE
I	COVE FILLER BLOCKS	16	1$\frac{1}{2}$ × 1$\frac{5}{8}$ × 5"	PINE
J	POST CAP	4	1 × 5$\frac{1}{2}$ × 5$\frac{1}{2}$"	EXTERIOR LUMBER
RAILING				
K	HANDRAIL	1	1$\frac{1}{2}$ × 5$\frac{1}{2}$ × 126$\frac{1}{2}$"	EXTERIOR LUMBER
L	STRETCHER RAILS	4	$\frac{3}{4}$ × 3$\frac{1}{2}$ × 126$\frac{1}{2}$"	EXTERIOR LUMBER
M	BALUSTERS	33	1$\frac{1}{2}$ × 1$\frac{1}{2}$ × 34$\frac{1}{2}$"	EXTERIOR LUMBER
N	MOUNTING BLOCK	4	1$\frac{1}{2}$ × 1$\frac{1}{2}$ × 3$\frac{1}{2}$"	EXTERIOR LUMBER
O	HANDRAIL MOUNTING BLOCK	4	1$\frac{1}{2}$ × 1$\frac{1}{2}$ × 2$\frac{1}{4}$"	EXTERIOR LUMBER
TRELLIS				
P	MOUNTING STRETCHERS	2	1$\frac{1}{2}$ × 2$\frac{1}{2}$ × 90$\frac{1}{2}$"	EXTERIOR LUMBER
Q	HORIZONTAL SLATS	10	$\frac{3}{4}$ × 1$\frac{1}{4}$ × 84"	EXTERIOR LUMBER
R	VERTICAL SLATS	13	1 × 1$\frac{1}{4}$ × 78"	EXTERIOR LUMBER
HARDWARE REQUIRED				
	FINISH NAILS		6d, 8d, 12d, 16d	
	DECK SCREWS		#8 × 2", #8 × 3"	

NOTICE: Part dimensions are based on ideal installation conditions. For best results, confirm measurements on actual project before cutting parts.

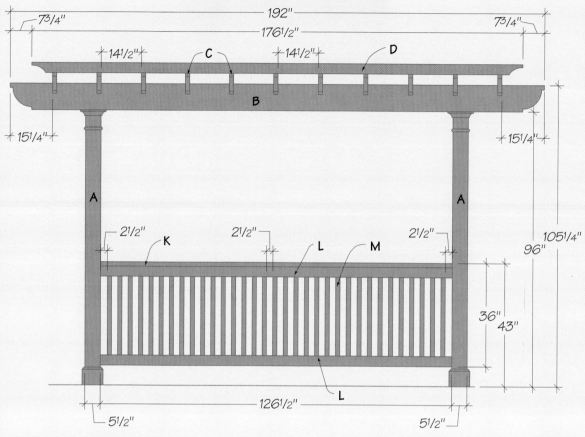

FRONT ELEVATION

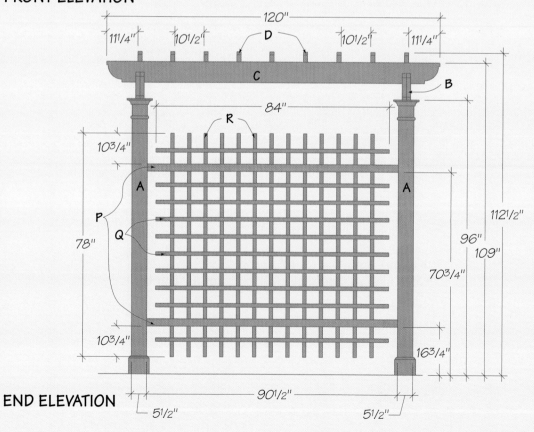

END ELEVATION

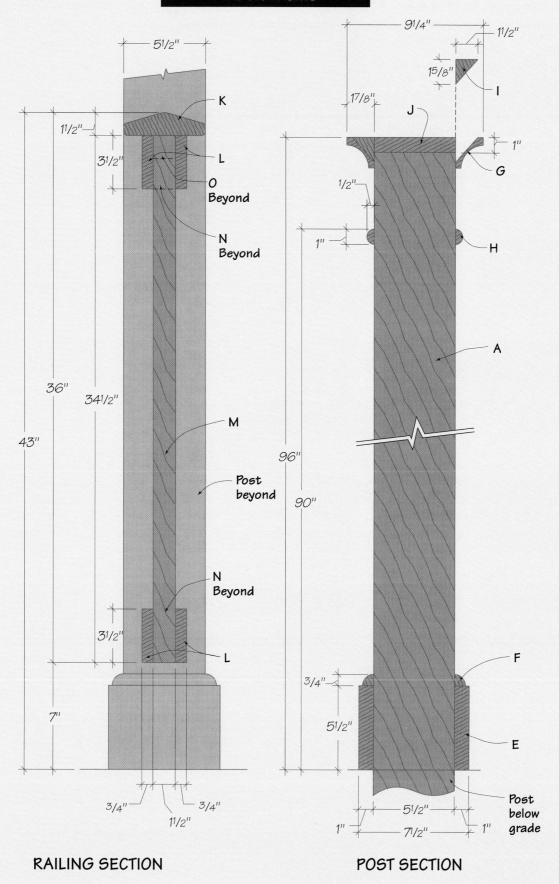

5 1/2"

K

1 1/2"

3 1/2"

L

O
Beyond

N
Beyond

36"

34 1/2"

43"

M

Post
beyond

N
Beyond

3 1/2"

L

7"

3/4"   3/4"

1 1/2"

RAILING SECTION

9 1/4"   1 1/2"

1 5/8"

I

1 7/8"

J

1"

G

1/2"

1"

H

A

96"

90"

3/4"

F

5 1/2"

E

Post
below
grade

5 1/2"

1"   7 1/2"   1"

POST SECTION

A pleasant refuge from the harsh sun is under the spreading, leafy branches of a tree. Unfortunately, it takes a tree years to mature enough to provide this kind of haven. An arbor structure, like this arbor/trellis, can provide a comparable escape after only a couple of weekends' work.

The arbor consists of four 6 × 6 posts supporting an open roof of beams and rafters. The open roof itself can screen and moderate the sun's rays, but it is really intended as a support for those spreading vines. The posts have been decorated with moldings, and the ends of the overhead beams and rafters have been sculpted with cove and ovolo shapes. To make the arbor more of an "outdoor room," you can add a railing or two and a trellis wall. These are the basic elements of an arbor/trellis structure. You can recombine them in other forms to meet your own needs.

Lay out the project area: A complete description of how to accomplish this using batter boards and masons' strings as guides can be found on pages 27 to 29. Once the layout is established, the strings will mark the

DETAIL 2: Use this profile drawing as a guide for laying out the hardboard ovolo template used to make the end profiles on the rafters and beams. For the rafters (made from 2 × 8s) enlarge the drawing 243% on a photocopier. For the beam ends (2 × 10s), enlarge the drawing 310%.

DETAIL 1: Cut the posts so they're a little longer than the finished height once they're set in concrete. Then, measure to the proper height on one of the posts and transfer the line to the other three posts using a line level and masons' string. Trim all posts to the same height with a circular saw.

outer edges of the posts. Mark each post hole with a spike or stake.

Dig the post holes. Your best bet probably is to use a clamshell-type post-hole digger (See page 11) to make the holes. For posts set in concrete, make the holes at least three times the width of the posts. In cold areas, the hole must extend below the frost line. If you're unsure of the frost line depth in your area, contact your local building inspector. Dig the holes deeper than required and backfill with 2 to 4 in. of gravel for drainage.

Cut each post longer than its finished height, including the depth of the hole. Set, brace and level the posts. After all posts are in place and the concrete has set, run a line level from post to post as a guide, then trim them to equal height with a circular saw *(See page 31 and Detail 1, above).* To prevent the tops of the posts from wicking moisture and rotting prematurely, cut post caps from ¾-in.-thick stock and attach them to the post tops with construction adhesive and deck screws. The edges of the caps should be flush with the edges of the posts.

Cut the parts. While the 10 ft. beams and 16

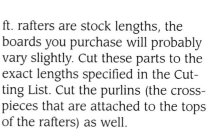
Line level

Masons' string

ft. rafters are stock lengths, the boards you purchase will probably vary slightly. Cut these parts to the exact lengths specified in the Cutting List. Cut the purlins (the crosspieces that are attached to the tops of the rafters) as well.

Shape the ends of the beams, rafters and purlins. To give the pergola a handsome, traditional appearance, the ends of the beams, rafters and purlins are trimmed to classic shapes—the ovolo (or quarter-round) on the beams and rafters, and a cove shape on the purlins. While it is possible to lay out the cuts from a pattern, then cut to the lines with a jigsaw, you'll get better, more consistent results if you use a router guided by a template to trim the ends. If you take this approach, you need to begin by making three templates from ¼-in.-thick hardboard. Use the drawing as a guide for the ovolo shapes *(See Detail 2)* and cut a simple cove in the ends of the purlins. Make rough cuts to within about ⅛ in. of the cutting lines using a jig saw, then smooth out the cuts (here is where the "production work" comes in to play) using a router with a 3-in. piloted pattern bit to follow the hardboard template. Adjust the cutting depth so the bearing rides along the edge of the template. Guiding the router along the template edge trims the work to match the template. After making the cuts, smooth the edges with a file and coarse sandpaper.

Erect the beams. Two beams support the overhead framing. Each beam is formed by two 2 × 10s, nailed together face to face. Each beam spans two posts. The first task in erecting the beams is to screw the 2 × 10s together with 2½ in. deck screws and construction adhesive. While the beams are still on the ground, lay out the locations of the rafters on the tops. Use a framing square to mark both beams at the same time *(See Detail 3).* With a helper and a pair of sturdy stepladders, lift the beams onto the posts and secure them by toe-nailing through the edges of the beams and into the post caps. If you prefer, you can use metal saddle fittings that fit onto the post tops. Tabs on the saddles are fastened to the beams with joist hanger nails. Once the beam is set onto the post, adjust it so the ends overhang the posts equally.

Notch the rafters to fit over the beams. The notch depth is not criti-

DETAIL 3: Use a framing square as a guide for gang-marking the rafter locations on top of the arbor/trellis beams. Follow the spacing shown in the drawing on page 88.

cal, as long as they are deep enough to securely lap the beams and not cut more than halfway through the rafters. We simply set the circular saw we used to cut the notches to its maximum cutting depth (2½ in.) then cut out the notches with multiple passes of the saw. Lay out the cuts first by ganging the rafters together face to face *(See Detail 4)* and using the spacing shown on page 88 as a guide. The ridges left in the bottom of the cut can be pared smooth with a chisel.

To hoist the rafters into place, begin by leaning them against one of the beams. On a stepladder, pull the rafters up and slide them across the beam until you can rest their ends on the far beam. To install a rafter, tip it on-edge and drop the notches over the beams. Toe-nail through the rafter into the beam *(See Detail 5).* Install all 11 rafters.

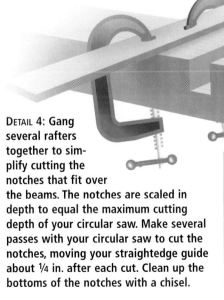

DETAIL 4: Gang several rafters together to simplify cutting the notches that fit over the beams. The notches are scaled in depth to equal the maximum cutting depth of your circular saw. Make several passes with your circular saw to cut the notches, moving your straightedge guide about ¼ in. after each cut. Clean up the bottoms of the notches with a chisel.

Install the purlins. The 2 × 4 purlins are installed much the same way as the rafters, except they aren't notched. Hoist the purlins up onto the rafters. Lay out position marks on the end rafters. One by one, roll the purlins on-edge, align them at the position marks and toe-nail them to the rafters.

While the posts can be left plain if you prefer, we added some decorative trim to enhance the traditional appearance of the arbor/trellis. The "post trim package" consists of a plain board, capped with a quarter-round molding, installed as a baseboard. Around the top of the post, we installed mitered 2-in. cove molding. Several inches below that is a half-round molding *(See Detail 6).* Trimming out each post is a straightforward matter of cutting four pieces of each element, with mitered ends, and nailing them to the post. Use stock moldings and

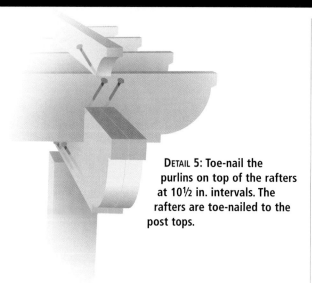

DETAIL 5: Toe-nail the purlins on top of the rafters at 10½ in. intervals. The rafters are toe-nailed to the post tops.

cut all the pieces to fit, one at a time (as opposed to cutting everything to a uniform measurement). Fasten the pieces with galvanized finish nails.

The railing shown with this project is completely optional. What it does is establish a boundary that can transform the arbor/trellis into an outdoor room or a gallery. The railing is quite simple to make and mount. Although we use square balusters, you could buy profiled deck balusters and use them instead. You can also alter the spacing of the balusters, but do not place them more than 4 in. apart. Cut the railing balusters to length from 2 × 2 stock. Set up a stopblock for your power miter saw or radial arm saw and cut all the pieces to the same size quickly and efficiently. Cut a few extra balusters. Also, save the short cutoff scraps.

INSTALLING COVE MOLDING

The only real complication encountered when trimming the posts involves the cove molding that attaches like crown molding at the top of each post. The primary hitch is the need to make and install "blocking" to support the molding. The size cove molding specified typically does not have a right-angle back. It is intended to be installed between a wall and a ceiling, so it has narrow flats to seat against wall and ceiling and a relieved back to bridge out-of-square seams. Since the molding won't seat against a ceiling, it needs back support. Measure and cut triangular blocking to provide the support. Also use the blocking as a jig when miter-cutting the cove molding to fit: with blocking behind it, orient the cove molding as if the fence of your saw were a "wall," the bottom of the molding resting on the saw table. This will create compound angle cuts that create perfect miter joints when the molding is installed.

You'll need at least four 2¼ in. pieces to help you space the balusters during assembly. These pieces later are used to mount the handrail. You also will need four 3½ in. pieces to use when mounting the railing assembly to the posts.

Cut the rails (both the stretcher rails and the handrail) to fit between the posts on the side or sides where the railing is installed. The handrail should be chamfered twice, so its top surface is peaked to shed water. It is easiest to do this cut with a stationary saw, such as a table saw or radial arm saw. It can, however, be done with a circular saw.

Assemble the stretchers and balusters. Begin by laying out three balusters and two of the stretcher rails. Position a baluster roughly at each end of the assembly, and one at dead center. Lay the stretcher rails on the balusters, one at the top, one at the bottom. Nail the rails to the center baluster. With the first baluster in place, slide two more balusters into position beneath the rails, one on either side. Use the 2¼-in.-long pieces of the baluster stock to space and align the balusters. Nail the new balusters in place. Keep adding balusters, using the spacer blocks to position the new ones, checking periodically to ensure that they are square to the rails. When all 33 balusters are nailed in place, turn the assembly over and set the second two stretcher rails in place. Align these rails and nail them to the balusters.

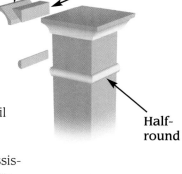

Mount the railing assembly. With some assistance from a helper, carry the railing assembly to the installation area. Clamp temporary supports to the posts and set the railing assembly in place. Slip a mounting block (a 3½-in.-long piece of 2 × 2) between the stretcher rails, align it so it is flush with the stretcher rails top and bottom and mark its location on the post. Do this at the top and bottom on both posts. Move the railing

DETAIL 6: Trim out the posts with decorative molding for a more elegant appearance. The cove molding, half-round molding and baseboard with quarter-round all are mitered at each corner.

assembly out of the way. Screw a mounting block to the posts at each marked location. Lift the assembly back into position. Drive nails through the stretcher rails into the mounting blocks. *(See Detail 7)*.

Mount the handrail. The spacer blocks you used to help assemble the railing are now used to mount the handrail. Set the handrail in place atop the upper stretcher rails. Select four spots for the mounting blocks and mark the handrail. Remove the handrail and screw the mounting blocks to the underside. Put the handrail back, settling the mounting blocks down between the stretcher rails. Drive nails through these rails into the mounting blocks.

We added a trellis to this project design to function as a screen, creating a bit of privacy without completely blocking the passage of light and breezes. It can, of course, support vines and other climbing plants. There are many options you could choose for trellising: you could create a three-walled room using trellising, railings or a combination of the two; you could trellis all four walls and create doorways in one or two of the trellis walls; or, you could make a walk-through by "walling" parallel sides. Cut the trellis parts. The trellis consists of two mounting rails, 10 horizontal slats and 13 vertical slats. Cut the parts to the dimensions specified in the Cutting List.

Fasten the vertical slats to the mounting rails. The slats, both vertical and horizontal, are located 6 in. apart, on center. Mark out the locations of the vertical slats on the mounting rails. On the vertical slats, mark the bottom edges of the two mounting rails. Pick a slat to get started. Apply a dot of construction adhesive and press the slat into place. Use a try square to ensure that the slat is perpendicular to the mounting rail, and check the alignment marks. Nail or screw the parts

Hand rail

Mounting blocks

DETAIL 7: 2 × 2 mounting blocks are attached to the posts to mount the stretcher rails and to the stretcher rails to mount the hand rail

together (if you own a pneumatic stapler, this is a perfect opportunity to use it). One by one, align the rest of the slats on the bottom mounting rail, making sure each is at right angles to the rail. Using a spacer made from scraps expedites this setup work. After all the slats are fastened to one rail, line up the second rail and fasten the slats to it.

Turn the trellis assembly over and attach the horizontal slats to the vertical slats and the rails. Use spacers to align the horizontal slats *(See Detail 8)*. The gap between the mounting rails and the adjacent horizontal slats is 4⅛ in. Cut a couple of scraps to that width. Lay them on the vertical slats, tight against one of the rails. Slide a horizontal slat against them and adjust its position end-to-end. Fasten this slat to each of the vertical slats. Use these same spacers to position and attach a slat on either side of both rails. Now cut a couple of spacers that are 4¾ in. wide. Use these in the same way to position the other horizontal slats.

Mount the trellis to the posts. Clamp scraps of wood to the posts where the mounting rails are to be attached. With a helper, lift the trellis into position and rest it on the clamped-in-place supports. Drill angled pilot holes through the rails into the posts. Drive a screw into each hole, securing the trellis to the posts. Unclamp the temporary supports.

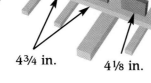

DETAIL 8: Use spacers as guides for installing the horizontal trellis slats. The gap between the outer slats and the rails is narrower than the gaps between inner slats.

4¾ in.   4⅛ in.

GARDEN STRUCTURES

The appeal of the garden is hard to capture in words. To the casual observer, it is far from glamorous: toiling in the dirt and weeds under the hot sun or in the cold and rain. But for those in the know, the appeal and the rewards are as obvious as they are hard to describe. Like any other pursuit, how well we enjoy the pleasures of gardening is greatly impacted by the tools we have at our disposal. And even though the basic "tools" for the gardener are quite simple—sun, dirt, seeds, a shovel and a watering can chief among them— adding a new garden structure, like a greenhouse or even a basic cold frame, opens up a whole new world of garden possibilities.

COMPOSTING PEN

This clever design makes a potentially unsightly structure a pleasant addition to your garden area—and it provides a great way to recycle organic wastes as fertilizer for your plants.

Cutting List

OVERALL DIMENSIONS (43 × 82½ × 37")

KEY	PART NAME	QTY.	SIZE	MATERIAL
SCREEN PANELS (PER UNIT, 7 UNITS REQUIRED)				
A	TOP/BOTTOM	2	1 × 3 × 36"	PRESSURE TREATED PINE
B	SIDE	2	1 × 3 × 34"	PRESSURE TREATED PINE
C	CORNER BLOCKS	4	1½ × 3½ × 3½"	PRESSURE TREATED PINE
BIN COMPONENTS				
D	POST ELEMENT	6	3½ × 3½ × 36⅞"	PRESSURE TREATED PINE
E	BRACES	2	1 × 2⅜ × 32⅝"	PRESSURE TREATED PINE
F	BRACES	2	1 × 2⅜ × 29⅞"	PRESSURE TREATED PINE
HARDWARE REQUIRED				
DECK SCREWS			#8 × 2½"	GALVANIZED
HOOKS & EYES		8	¼ × 2½"	
FENCING (OR POULTRY) STAPLES			¾"	
WIRE MESH FENCING			36" × 25'-roll	

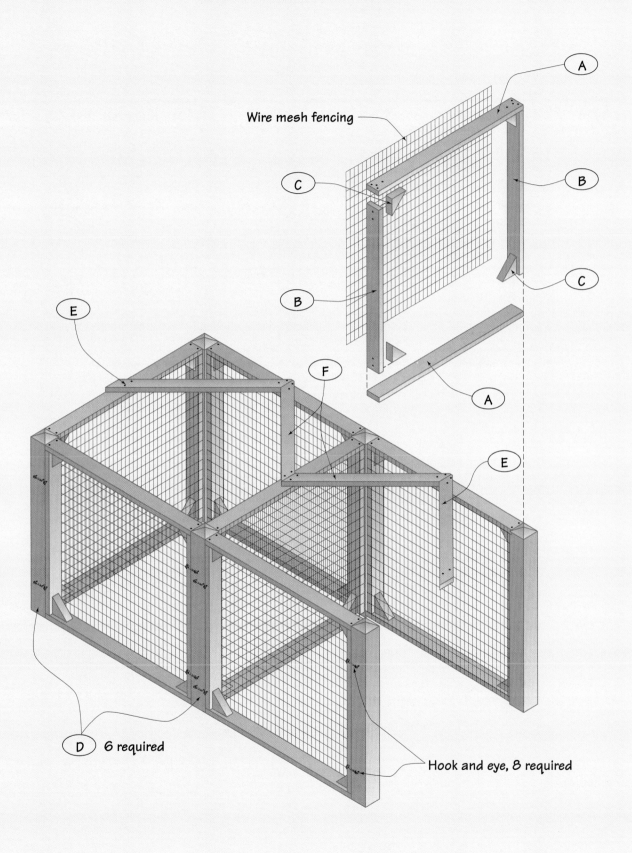

Wire mesh fencing

A

B

C

C

B

E

F

E

D 6 required

Hook and eye, 8 required

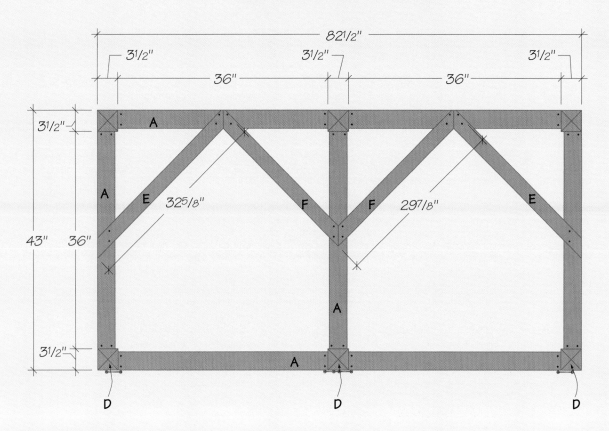

82¹/₂"

3¹/₂" 3¹/₂" 3¹/₂"

36" 36"

3¹/₂"

A

A E 32⁵/₈" F F 29⁷/₈" E

43" 36"

A

3¹/₂"

A

D D D

PLAN VIEW

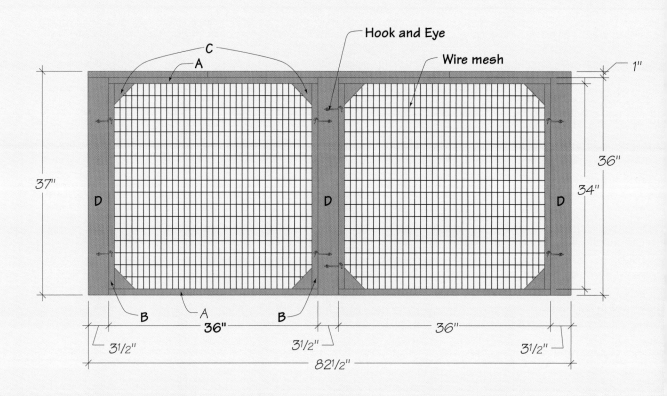

Hook and Eye

C

A Wire mesh

1"

D D D 36"

37" 34"

B A B

36" 36"

3¹/₂" 3¹/₂" 3¹/₂"

82¹/₂"

M aintaining an attractive, tidy yard with healthy shrubs and trees, beautiful flowers and a lush lawn can produce a mountain— well, at least more than a mole-hill—of garden trash like grass clippings, pruning cutoffs and leaves. The costs of landfilling all this good organic material are driving many homeowners to turn back to an old-time solution: composting. Given some time and a little encouragement (in the form of shredding and periodic turning), those garden and yard wastes can be transformed into a nutrient-rich soil amendment. It doesn't take a lot of work on your part to produce compost, but it does require some forbearance. If you value tidiness and attractiveness, the vision of a loose, unsightly heap of decomposing organic matter is off-putting.

But here's a solution: This composting pen allows you to tidy up that pile, and in the bargain, organize and structure this practical garden process. The structure shown has two cubicles. But the modular nature of the construction makes it easy to expand into a three- or four-cubicle unit.

Once assembled, the composting pen can be carried by two people, so it doesn't have to be permanently sited. But if you think it appropriate, you can anchor it to the ground with foot-long pieces of rebar driven through the frames into the ground.

Make the posts & screen frames

Cut the 4 × 4 posts that support the screens. To improve the appearance of the composting pen and to prevent pooling on the post tops, we beveled the post tops on all four sides. There are several ways this can be accomplished: we used a power miter saw (*See Photo 1*). After cutting the frame pieces to size, save the cutoff pieces to make the 28 corner blocks needed for the screens.

Photo 1 Bevel all four sides of each post top at a 45° angle. A power miter saw is an excellent tool for this task. Set up the saw and position the workpiece so the blade exits at the midpoint of the post end.

Photo 2 Attach the frame tops and bottom to the sides using construction adhesive and galvanized deck screws to fortify the joint. Be sure to drill pilot holes before driving the screws.

The 3-in.-wide stock for the tops, bottoms and sides is ripped to width from 5⁄4 × 6-in. stock (actual size is approximately 1 × 5¼ in.), which is usually made for use as deck boards. Some of the narrow strips left over from ripping can be used to make the diagonal braces installed later. After ripping the stock, cross-cut the screen frame parts to length.

The four strips making up each frame are joined together with construction adhesive and galvanized deck screws. Apply a modest bead of adhesive to the end of a side, and butt the overlapping top or bottom against it. Drill pilot holes and drive two screws into the joint *(See Photo 2).*

When the basic frames are assembled and squared, cut the

Photo 3 Corner blocks cut from the cutoff pieces of the frame strengthen each frame and help keep it from falling out of square. Attach the corner blocks with construction adhesive and deck screws driven through the frame and into the blocks.

Photo 4 Apply a finish to the posts and frames before attaching the mesh. The finish improves the appearance of the project and also helps extend its life by protecting the wood.

NOTICE: We used pressure-treated pine to build this project. It is an inexpensive building material that withstands ongoing exposure to moisture and insect infestation. And when painted or treated (we used a redwood-colored, UV-resistant wood stain) it can be as attractive as any other exterior wood. But because the chemicals used to treat the lumber are potentially health threatening, you should take plenty of precautions when handling pressure-treated stock. The greatest hazard is created by sawdust generated when the wood is cut, so always wear a particle mask when sawing or drilling treated lumber. Also wear gloves when handling it and clean up sawdust and cutoff scraps immediately. Do not burn any wood or sawdust that has been pressure-treated.

Photo 5 Use masking tape to mark cutting lines on the metal mesh. The mesh used here is a galvanized product with ½ in. grids sold in 36-in.-wide rolls.

Photo 6 Attach the mesh to the fronts of the frames with fencing staples. These galvanized fasteners are sometimes called U-nails. Drive a staple every 6 in. along each side of the frame. Make sure no cut wires extend past the edges of the frame.

corner blocks. Apply adhesive to one of the corner blocks and press it firmly into an inside corner. Drill pilot holes and drive screws through the frame members and into the angled edges of the block, drawing the blocks tight (See Photo 3). Assemble all seven frames.

If you are going to paint or stain the compost bin, the time to do it is before the mesh is attached. You'll be able to get finishing materials onto all the surfaces and edges. We applied redwood-colored UV-protected wood stain to the parts (See Photo 4).

Cut seven 3-ft.-square pieces of the wire mesh. We used 36-in.-wide rolls of galvanized wire mesh with ½ in. grids. To mark the mesh for cutting, lay a frame on top of it and apply masking tape at the cutting point (See Photo 5). Cut the mesh to length with aviator snips. Use aviator snips. Make the cuts as close as possible to a crosswire in the mesh, so you don't have sharp ends jutting out. Using fencing staples (galvanized U-shaped nails), attach a piece of mesh to each of the wooden frames (See Photo 6). The middle divider has mesh on both sides of the frame.

Assemble the composting pen

Select a frame and clamp a post to each side. The bottoms of the posts should be flush with the bottom of the frame. Drill pilot holes and drive screws through the frame sides into the posts (See Photo 7). Make up two more subassemblies like this one—a frame with a post attached to each side. Use one of the remaining frames to connect two of the subassemblies. Clamp the frame to a post in each subassembly, align these parts, then screw them together. Clamp another frame to the assembly and screw it in place at the third post-and-frame subassembly (See Photo 8). When you are through, you will have two bins that are connected and open in the front.

Mount the removable frames. These provide access to the bins so you can turn the composting materials easily, or reach in to shovel the compost out once it has decomposed sufficiently. Each of these frames is held in place with four ordinary hook-and-eye latches. Stand the removable frames in the openings in the assembly and clamp them to the posts. Drill pilot holes, then screw the hooks into the posts near each corner.

Photo 7 Attach the frame between posts with galvanized deck screws. Make sure the bottoms of the frames align with the bottoms of the posts.

Photo 8 Complete the post-and-frame assembly by driving screws into the last frame and into a shared corner post. You can do this step in your construction area or move the assembly parts on site and join them together there.

Mark the spots where the screw eyes fall onto the frames, then drill holes and attach the screw eyes *(See Photo 9 and Photo 10)*.

Mount the diagonal braces at the top corners of the cubicles. The braces simply stiffen the unit and keep the sides from flexing in and out. Miter one end of each of the four cutoff strips of 5/4 deck board left over from ripping the frame stock. Lay the braces in place on the tops of the bins and mark the cuts to be made to the other ends *(See Photo 11)*. Trim the braces to the cutting lines, then screw them to the bins.

Install the composting pen in your yard. Choose an inconspicuous site that is convenient to your gardening areas. Avoid installing the pen near any permanent structures (the one built here is fairly attractive compared or other designs, but little can be done about the odors that can be created). To help keep the pen stationary, drill holes in the bottom frames on each end and drive a 12-in.-long section of rebar through each hole and into the ground *(See Photo 12)*.

Using the composting pen

Raw materials for the compost can be accumulated in one cubicle. After you mow your grass, empty the clippings into one of the units. After weeding the garden, thinning plants, pruning shrubs and bushes, add the accumulated organic waste to the clippings. Even compostable kitchen scraps can be added to the compost recipe. Periodically, open up the front of the bin and shred the decomposing material. The newly shredded material is then transferred into the second cubicle. Before long, it is broken down by microbial activity and is ready to be spread in the garden.

Photo 9 Attach the screw eye hooks to the posts first, then mark the spots where they fall across the posts with a pencil. Attach the eyebolts for the screw eyes at these spots. The screw eyes hold the removable frames in place but allow you to remove them easily for turning or removing compost.

Photo 10 Make sure the screw eyes at the center post are far enough apart that they do not interfere with one another.

Photo 11 Lay the mitered frame braces across the tops of the bins and scribe cutting lines at the free ends using a combination square. The braces greatly increase the sturdiness and wrack-resistance of the composting pen. Apply a finish to the frame braces before attaching them with screws.

Photo 12 Stake the composting pen in place by driving 12-in.-long pieces of rebar through holes drilled in the bottom frame pieces near each end of the unit.

COLD FRAME

A cold frame lets you get a jump on the growing season come spring or even prolong your fall harvest. In just an afternoon, you can use this plan to turn an old window sash and a sheet of plywood into a versatile, portable cold frame.

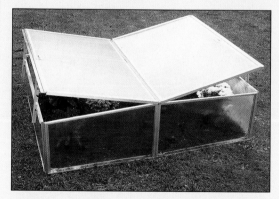

OPTION: BUY A COLD FRAME KIT

If you'd rather not build your cold frame from scratch, you can build one using a pre-fabricated kit instead. The one shown here is composed entirely of precut parts that come ready to assemble. The light panels are made of polycarbonate plastic, and the framework is aluminum. Kit-built cold frames come in a number of shapes and styles, but the primary difference between them is the number of light panels that open up for plant access.

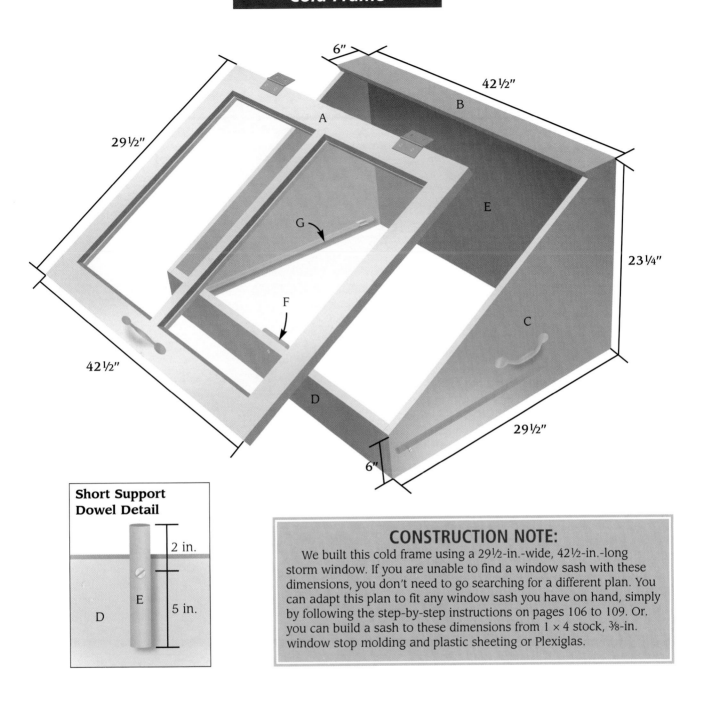

6"

42½"

B

29½"

A

G

E

23¼"

F

C

42½"

D

29½"

6"

**Short Support
Dowel Detail**

2 in.

E

5 in.

D

CONSTRUCTION NOTE:
We built this cold frame using a 29½-in.-wide, 42½-in.-long storm window. If you are unable to find a window sash with these dimensions, you don't need to go searching for a different plan. You can adapt this plan to fit any window sash you have on hand, simply by following the step-by-step instructions on pages 106 to 109. Or, you can build a sash to these dimensions from 1 × 4 stock, ⅜-in. window stop molding and plastic sheeting or Plexiglas.

Cutting List

OVERALL DIMENSIONS (42½ × 29½ × 23¼")

KEY	PART NAME	QTY.	SIZE	MATERIAL
A	WINDOW SASH	1	1⅛ × 29½ × 42½"	N/A
B	TOP	1	¾ × 6 × 41"	EXTERIOR PLYWOOD
C	SIDES	2	¾ × 29½ × 23¼"	"
D	FRONT	1	¾ × 6 × 41"	"
E	BACK	1	¾ × 41 × 22½"	"
F	SHORT SUPPORT	1	¾-DIA. × 7"	HARDWOOD DOWEL
G	LONG SUPPORTS	2	¾-DIA. × 26½"	HARDWOOD DOWEL

In the project shown here we use an old storm window sash of a specific size to build a cold frame. However, these step-by-step instructions are designed so that you can build your cold frame with a sash of any size.

1 Measure the length, width and thickness of your window sash. Record these dimensions.

2 Determine how wide to make the side panels for the cold frame. Starting from one corner of a sheet of ¾-in. exterior plywood, measure off the width of the sash along the bottom edge of the plywood and make a mark. Draw a 2-ft.-long perpendicular line from this mark using a carpenter's square as a guide. This line represents the back edge of the side panel.

Back-of-side-panel line (about 2 ft. long)

3 Draw a reference line 6 in. to the left of the back-of-side-panel line. Both lines should be parallel and the same length.

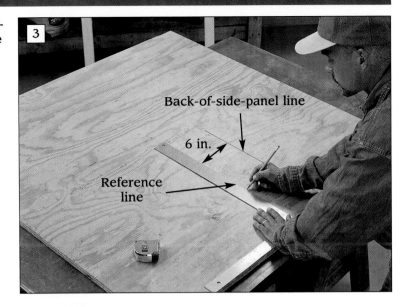

Back-of-side-panel line

6 in.

Reference line

4 Lay out the sloping edge of the side panel. Start by measuring 6 in. up from the lower left corner of the plywood to mark where the bottom of the slope begins. The top of this sloped line intersects the reference line you drew in Step 3. To find this point of intersection, subtract 1 in. from the width of your sash. Using a metal rule, measure out that amount (sash width minus 1 in.) and pivot the rule at the bottom-of-the-slope point until it intersects with the reference line. Connect the top and bottom slope points with a straight line.

Lay out the top of the side panel: Draw a line from the top of the sloped line over to the back-of-side-panel line to mark the top of the panel. This line should be parallel to the bottom edge of the side panel.

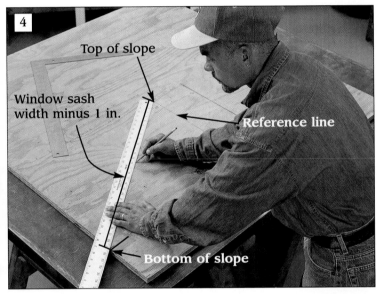

Top of slope

Window sash width minus 1 in.

Reference line

Bottom of slope

5 Lay out cutting lines for the sash on the side panel. Notice in the drawing on page 105 that the sash fits into a notch at the top of the side panels. To mark for this notch, draw a short line in from the top of the sloped line. Use a square to make this short line perpendicular to your sloped line and as long as your sash is thick. At the bottom of this sash notch line, draw a second line parallel to the sloped top line back to the left edge of the plywood. When you cut out the side panel, you'll cut along the sash notch line and the inside sloped line.

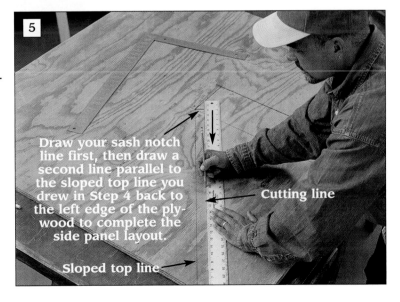

Draw your sash notch line first, then draw a second line parallel to the sloped top line you drew in Step 4 back to the left edge of the plywood to complete the side panel layout.

Cutting line

Sloped top line

6 Cut out the side panel using a jig saw and a straightedge guide. Be sure to cut the sloped edge along the cutting line you drew in Step 5, not the original top slope reference line.

Use this first side panel as a pattern to trace the other side onto a piece of plywood, then cut out the second side.

Cutting line for sloped edge

7 Measure and cut the front, top and back pieces. The length of the these parts should be equal to the length of your sash, less 1½ in. Both the front and top are 6 in. wide. One long edge of the front must be beveled to correspond with the sloped edges of the sides. The top must also be beveled along one edge to match the sash notch angle. The other long edges of the front and top are square. Use the side panels as a reference for determining the bevels you'll need to cut on the top and front. Then rip the front and top pieces to width with a circular saw set at the appropriate bevel angles. Cross-cut the parts to length.

Rip and cross-cut the back panel to size. Its length should be 1½ in. shorter than your sash length. The width of the back is ¾ in. shorter than the height of the sides.

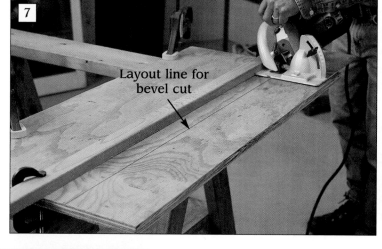

Layout line for bevel cut

8 Glue and screw the cold frame together. Assemble the back and side panels first. Run a bead of moisture-resistant wood glue along the ends of the back, set it in between the side panels and fasten the parts with countersunk 1½-in. galvanized deck screws. A couple of wood screws clamped to the bottom edges of the sides make it easy to stand the sides upright while you fasten the parts together.

To complete the box assembly, attach the top and front panels between the sides with glue and screws, making sure the beveled edges are correctly oriented on the side panels.

Prime all inside and outside surfaces of the cold frame box, then topcoat with two coats of exterior-grade latex paint.

9 Attach the long lid supports: Cut the long dowel supports so they're about 3 in. shorter than the width of the cold frame. Hold each dowel 1 in. up from the inside, bottom edges of the side panels. Drill a pilot hole 1 in. from the ends of the dowels closest to the cold frame front and through the side panels. Slip a bolt through each pilot hole and fasten with a washer and locknut to hold the dowels in place while allowing them to pivot. Install broom clips to the side panels near the opposite ends of the dowels to hold them in place when not in use.

Install the short lid support. This support, mounted to the front of the cold frame, holds the sash open at two settings for ventilation. Cut a 7-in. length of ¾-in.-dia. dowel, and mark it 2 in. from one end. Position the dowel so the 2-in. mark is about 1 in. below the top edge of the front panel, centered from side to side. Drill a pilot hole through the dowel where you've marked it and through the front panel. Install the dowel with a bolt and nut. When you pivot the dowel one way or the other, it will hold the sash open either 1 in. or 4 in.

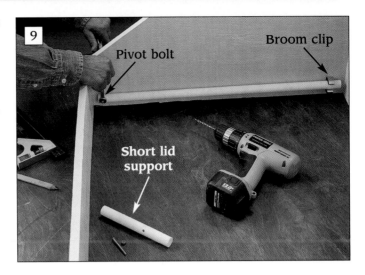

Pivot bolt

Broom clip

Short lid support

10 Fasten 3-in. lift handles to the side panels of the box and to the lower rail of the sash. Refer to the drawing on page 105 for general placement of the handles, and be sure to use galvanized or brass handles and screws. Place them so the cold frame balances comfortably when you lift it up.

Install the sash. Attach two hinges to the top of the sash, about 6 in. from each end. We used 3-in. galvanized butt hinges, but brass hinges would work, too. Set the sash in place on the cold frame, and fasten the hinges to the top of the cold frame.

11 Drill lid support holes in the sash. The long lid supports fit into 1-in.-dia. holes drilled ¼ in. deep into the bottom of the sash. The holes hold the lid supports securely to prop the sash open. To mark the sash frame for the holes, simply prop the sash open and trace around the ends of the supports. Drill the holes with a Forstner bit in a drill/driver.

GREENHOUSE

The crown jewel in any gardener's crown, a personal greenhouse opens up countless new possibilities for the true gardening enthusiast. And when built from a kit, like the one above, they're a snap to build.

Greenhouse Project: *A 3-step overview*

Assemble the frame (113 to 117)

Install panels & roof vents (118 to 120)

Hang the door (120 to 121)

In addition to the freestanding greenhouse featured in this chapter, you can also find kits for greenhouses that are attached to your house (left) or are designed to cover a deck or patio (above).

GREENHOUSE ACCESSORIES

Part of the fun of building a greenhouse is customizing it by adding a few unique bells and whistles. Kit manufacturers can get you started down this trail with a few optional devices.

A hydraulic lifter activated by changes in temperature can keep your greenhouse from turning into a steamroom if it gets warm outside and you're not around to manually open the vents. As the temperature rises, the hydraulic oil expands and lifts the vent.

This photo shows a louvered exhaust fan that can be wired to a "smart" thermometer. If the temperature in the greenhouse rises above a predetermined level, the thermometer signals the exhaust fan to kick in and vent the hot air. Another type of thermometer (seen at the far right of the photo) records the minimum and maximum temperature in the greenhouse on a day-to-day basis.

Kit manufacturers and many nurseries also sell shelves, racks and tables designed for use in a greenhouse.

Floor options for greenhouses

Loose fill such as bark or landscaping rock is a suitable floor material for most light-use greenhouses. You'll still need to provide a frame or curb to contain the material and anchor the structure.

The paver-and-landscape-timber foundation used in our featured project is made by bolting four landscaping timbers together, then setting pavers into a bed of sand, as you would for any paver patio project. In addition to its attractive appearance and durability, the hard surface make it practical and easy for the homeowners to run power service to their greenhouse.

GREENHOUSE KITS

Of the many yard and garden structures for which kits are available, greenhouses may make the most sense. The typical built-from-scratch greenhouse (with its inevitable broken glass panels or cloudy, unappealing plastic) can't compete with the durability and appearance of the high-strength polycarbonate panels featured in most quality greenhouse kits. And after all, a greenhouse is really nothing more than a skeleton that supports a see-through skin.

The greenhouse parts are delivered packaged in just a couple of elongated cardboard boxes. Don't tear open all the packaging! The parts for each subassembly—the gable-end walls, the side walls and so forth—are bundled together. You can avoid confusion by leaving each bundle intact and unopened until you are actually ready to assemble the parts.

Every gardener worth his or her mulch has wished for a greenhouse at one time or another. For the handyman, a small greenhouse project seems eminently do-able. Seems do-able, that is, until you get deep into designing the framing and sorting through the glazing options. Then it looks awfully complicated.

At that point, a greenhouse kit looks better and better. All the vexing decisions involving materials choices have been made. The design will have been tested and proven. All you have to do is spend a weekend assembling the parts, then the gardener in you can cut loose.

The greenhouse kit we selected is the Danish-made *Juliana* model, distributed in this country by *GardenStyles* of Bloomington, Minnesota. The greenhouse has virtually unbreakable polycarbonate glazing panels that mount in a framework of extruded aluminum members. Everything is cut to precise (metric) measurements. With a little help, you can easily assemble and glaze the unit in a weekend.

In a nutshell, the process is to assemble each of the walls before setting any of them up. The structure is light enough that any wall

Photo 1:1 To avoid confusion, wait until you're ready to assemble each wall section before opening the bundle containing the parts to make the section. Check the parts against the inventory as you lay them out in roughly the sequence they're installed.

can be lifted and carried by one person. You set up the walls, then add the roof framing and the roof-vent frames. Then the entire unit is glazed, the door is hung and the structure is anchored to its foundation.

Site preparation is minimal. You'll probably want to remove sod from the site, and it should be level and reasonably well compacted. But this is an easy job, because you don't need to set up batterboards and run lines outlining the perimeter. The foundation almost sites itself. For the project shown here, the homeowner chose to install a loose-paver floor framed with landscape timbers *(See page 112).*

SECURING YOUR GREENHOUSE TO THE FOUNDATION

When preparing your construction site, take into account that the greenhouse will need to be fastened somehow to the earth. If you're laying a paver or loose-fill foundation, install landscape timbers around the perimeter of the construction area (See Photo, previous page) so you can simply screw the greenhouse sill plates to the timbers (See Photo, left). Normally, this is done after the kit is completely assembled. Drill holes through the sill and drive 3-in. screws through the holes into the wood. If you're pouring a concrete slab to support the greenhouse, insert threaded J-bolts (See page 29) into the fresh concrete. Position the J-bolts so the greenhouse sill plates will be centered on top of them.

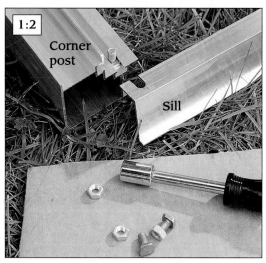

Photo 1:2 Mechanical fasteners are used to join the frame members. Here, square-headed bolts fit into T-slots in the corner post. An open slot on the sill is fitted over the threaded end of the bolt.

Photo 1:3 Diagonal braces are fastened across the struts that function as studs in the front wall frames surrounding the door opening. The braces make the walls more rigid, which is especially useful on the front wall due to stress from opening and closing the door to the greenhouse.

Photo 1:4 Connecting plates are used to join the rafters together at the peak.

Photo 1:5 "L"-angled connector plates join the rafters and the corner posts at the eave area of the greenhouse. The ends of the braces are attached to the same "L" connector on the post.

Photo 1:6 Install the door header between the tallest struts in the front wall.

Photo 1:7 Once the front wall is completed, assemble the side walls, back wall and back wall gable one at a time.

ONE: Assemble the framing

Start assembly of the frame walls with the front wall, then build the side and back walls. After all walls are complete, erect them and join them together.

Front wall: Unpack the parts for the front wall and practice arranging them according to the diagram in the assembly instructions *(See Photo 1:1).* By laying out the parts in the proper arrangement, you'll see what needs to be done. Each part in the drawing is numbered, and that number is printed on the actual part in the bundle. The instructions include small drawings of each connection that must be made to assemble this wall, so consult them wherever a detail isn't immediately obvious.

As you study the instructions for assembling the front wall, you will see there's a sequence suggested. This general sequence can be followed when building the side walls and back wall as well.

• Begin assembly at the bottom left corner of each wall frame, connecting the sill to the corner post *(See Photo 1:2).*

• Move across the sill, installing diagonal metal braces that connect the struts ("struts" correspond to wall studs). *(See Photo 1:3)*

• Next, the two rafters are joined together at the peak, using a special plate—it will be marked. Slide this unit into position so it can be joined with angle plates to the two corner posts *(See Photo 1:4).*

• Connect the corner posts to the sill by bolting an angle plate and horizontal and diagonal braces to the post *(See Photo 1:5).*

• Connect horizontal braces to the doorway studs, then add the door header *(See Photo 1:6).*

With a sense of direction established, break out the bolts and nuts and begin connecting the parts. You'll see immediately that each strut has a continuous slot formed into it to accommodate a bolt head.

Photo 1:8 Begin erecting the wall frames. Start with the back wall and one of the side walls. The frames are lightweight, but you'll need two people to connect them.

Photo 1:9 The side walls and gable walls are joined at shared corner posts. The side walls are connected to the corner posts with screws.

1:10

Photo 1:10
After all four walls are erected, raise the ridge pole and fit the ends into the open "V's" formed at the tops of the front and back gable peaks. With the green-house model shown here, the pole has flanges that fit into slots in the rafters. You'll need to flex each wall outward momen-tarily to slip the pole into place. Make sure your ladders are set up on firm ground.

Mating parts have either holes or notch-like slots for the bolts. Thus the connection points are pretty obvious. Alignment adjustments are made by moving the bolt in the slot. As you join the parts, thread nuts onto the bolts and tighten them with a nut driver.

You should note that the sills and corner posts don't meet in a closed corner; instead there's a gap or notch, which is for the side wall's sill. The same is true at the joint between the corner post and the rafters. An angled plate is bolted first to the corner post. A cross brace and a diagonal brace go on the bolts that secure the plate to the post. After the door and wall posts and the braces are all secure, you bolt the rafters to the corner post via the angled plate. A gap is to be left between post and rafter, so the side wall's top plate, which doubles as a rain gutter, can link into place.

Don't worry too much about getting all the parts perfectly aligned and squared up at this point. The wall will take shape and assume a reasonable rough alignment as you bolt the parts together, and that's all you need to focus on at this point. Later, as the walls are set up and joined together, the alignment will become more refined. And installing the glazing will force everything into perfect alignment.

For now, bear in mind that you may need to loosen a few nuts to allow parts to shift so one wall can be connected to its neighbor. In other words, you don't need to tighten the nuts "for the ages," you just may need to loosen them to make slight adjustments after they are installed.

The other walls are assembled one by one. Just do one at a time, and don't open a bundle of parts until you are going to assemble them. Lay out the parts according to the diagram in the manufacturer's assembly instructions. It is reasonable to follow the same general sequence you'll follow when assembling the front wall. Start at the lower left corner of the layout and work your way up and across the unit, roughly aligning them and bolting the parts together.

The rear gable wall closely approximates the front wall—it simply lacks the doorway. The side walls are composed of only seven pieces, and they lack corner posts (*See Photo 1:7*). This is because the gable walls contain the structure's corner posts.

Erect the wall frames. Lift the rear gable wall and stand it on the foundation. While your helper holds

Photo 1:11
Fasten the
rafters to the
ridgepole and
the side wall
sills. The holes
and slots are
predrilled so you
don't need to
worry about
spacing the
parts.

1:11

that wall, lift a side wall and bring it into position (See Photo 1:8). The sill and plate of the side wall fit into the spaces left for them in the gable wall. While you should get a good fit at the sills, you may need to loosen some of the bolts in the gable walls to adjust the space for the plate/gutter. Attach the side wall to the back wall post (See Photo 1:9). After the first side wall is locked in place, connect the second side wall to the gable wall.

Erect the front gable wall last. The other three walls should be pretty much self-supporting, so you and your helper can each take a side of the rear wall and get it tied into the structure quickly.

Install the roof frame. The primary roof member is the ridge. The heads of the mounting bolts catch in slots in the undersides of the rafters, and the bolt shanks pass through short slots cut in the flange on the bottom of the ridge.

Thread a nut on a bolt, catch the head in the rafter's slot and slip the bolt a couple of inches down the slot. Turn the nut finger tight, just to hold the bolt in place. Do this with one bolt at each rafter. Set up stepladders inside the greenhouse, one at each gable wall. You

hold one end of the ridge, and a helper holds the other end. You both go up the ladders, lift the ridge up and clear of the structure, then lower it into place (See Photo 1:10). One of you probably will need to push the rafters out a bit so the ridge can drop into place, with the flange beneath the rafters. Pull the rafters tight against the ridge, and the bolts can be slid up the slot and right into the niches cut for them in the ridge's flange. Tighten the nuts with a nut driver, and the ridge is secure.

Struts, which correspond to rafters in a stick-framed roof, are installed next (See Photo 1:11). The locations for the struts are clearly indicated by holes bored in the ridge's flange. You slip a bolt into the continuous slot in the strut, lay the strut's end on top of the ridge flange and the bolt shank will drop through the hole in the flange. Thread on the nut and tighten it. At the lower end, the struts bolt to the side wall top plate in the same way.

Photo 2:1 Slip the rubber gasket that holds the top edge of the roof panel over the ridgepole flange at the top of each roof panel opening. Also snap a gasket into the bottom edge of each roof panel.

Photo 2:2 After securing the top edge of the roof panel in the gasket at the top of the opening, flex the panel and snap the bottom edge in position. The sides should rest on the rafter ledges.

TWO: Install the panels & roof vents

The greenhouse is glazed with special polycarbonate panels. Polycarbonate is the plastic used in safety goggles; it is virtually unbreakable. The panels have a corrugated core, which provides insulation value. The outside of the panel has a UV coating to retard the degradation of the material from the sun's ultraviolet radiation.

When you unpack the glazing, you'll see that each panel is cut to a precise size to fit specific openings in the framework. No cutting is necessary. A protective film masks the panels to protect them from scratching during shipping and installation.

There are two methods for securing the panels into the building frame (and other kit manufacturers have their own altogether different approaches). One way is to bond the panels into the frames with silicone caulk, then secure them with spring-wire clips that are fitted into the frame channel, locking the panel into place. In effect, the clips "clamp" the panel in place until the caulk sets, bonding the panel.

The greenhouse kit we installed featured a somewhat newer technology for installing the polycarbonate panels. Instead of caulk and spring clips, semi-rigid plastic gaskets are snapped in place over the panel frames to immobilize the panels within the frames.

The assembly instructions should provide a diagram so you can easily determine which panels are used where. Snap a rubber gasket onto the ridgepole flange at the top of the outer panel openings *(See Photo 2:1)*. Also attach a rubber gasket to the bottom edge of each panel. Then, fit the top edge of each panel into the rubber gasket at the top of the correct panel opening *(See Photo 2:2)*. Fit the bottom edge into the top side wall sill (you'll probably need to flex the panel slightly to do this). The sides of the panel should rest on the rafter ledges at the sides of the panel openings. Fit the plastic outer gaskets over the top ridges on the rafters and snap them down to pin the sides of the panels in place *(See Photo 2:3)*.

As you work, you may discover that here and there you need to loosen an assembly bolt or two to adjust the align-

Photo 2:3 Snap the plastic gaskets over the rafters to press the panels snugly against the rafter ledges.

Photo 2:4 After installing the shorter fixed panels in the interior roof openings, frame out each opening to accept a roof vent.

Photo 2:5 Assemble the roof vents. The vent frames are wide enough to span two panel openings. To assemble them, install the polycarbonate panels and attach the support rods that are used to prop the vents in an open position.

2:6

Photo 2:6 Slip the top rail of each roof vent assembly into the channel near the top of the ridgepole (See inset photo), then slide the vents into position. The lips at the side edges of the vent panels should fit over the tops of the rafters.

ment of the frame so a panel will fit its opening.

The upper third or so of each inner roof panel opening is covered with an operating vent window. Before assembling the windows, install the shorter fixed panels in the lower two-thirds of each opening, then install the top frame that separates the fixed and vented panels in the openings (*See Photo 2:4*).

To assemble and install the vented windows, first unbundle the parts and lay them out. As with other components, the assembly is pretty clearcut. Slip bolts through the predrilled holes, joining the parts together, and tighten the nuts. After the vent frames are assembled, bolt a prop to each one (*See Photo 2:5*). Install the panels into the openings.

The vents are hinged by means of interlocking grooves formed in both the ridgepole and the vent-frame hinge rail. The vent is slid into place from one end of the ridge (*See Photo 2:6*).

GREENHOUSE Step Three: Hang the door

3:1

Photo 3:1 Assemble the door that came with your kit, in this case by screwing the corners together (all holes are predrilled and all hardware provided). Attach the hinges and door latch.

THREE: Hang the door

Open up the door bundle and lay out the parts. It will looks like an aluminum storm-and-screen door, complete with a lever-type latch with a lock. Holes for the assembly screws are already drilled. All you have to do is drive the screws to assemble the door.

Four hinges are provided. The leaves with the pins are attached to the doorpost, while the leaves with the sockets are installed on the door (*See Photo 3:1*).

The latch mechanism fits into the door stile, and the lever is screwed to the stile surface.

The polycarbonate panels in the door shown here were installed using a different method from the one described in the previous sec-

Photo 3:2 The door panels in this kit were installed using a slightly different system than was used to install the roof panels. The first step is simply to line the frame opening with silicone caulk.

Photo 3:3 Press each panel into the bed of silicone in the frame opening. Then, insert spring clips between the panels and the frame ledges to secure the door panels.

tion. They required the silicone-and-spring-clamp method discussed on page 118.

For the best bond, the panels and the aluminum frame need to be dry. For this reason, the distributor recommends that you keep the glazing panels on the cardboard packing rather than laying them on the grass. Wipe the adjoining surfaces with acetone to remove any grease or solvents. You don't need to scrub the surfaces; a quick pass with a soft rag dampened with acetone will do the trick. But to clean the edges of the panels, you need to peel the masking from the inside surface. The blue-colored masking identifies the surface with the UV coating.

Run a bead of caulk around each frame opening (See Photo 3:2). Then, set the panels into the appropriate frame openings. Snap spring clips between the panels and the tops of the frame flanges to hold them in place (See Photo 3:3). After the panels are installed, hang the door onto the pins to mount it to the greenhouse.

Install any trim pieces or additional accessories, like plastic end caps for the ridge and sill or a door catch to hold the door open (See Photo 3:4).

Photo 3:4 Hang the door with the hinges provided and test the operation. Then, mount the door catch to the door frame and the front wall frame so the door can be held in an open position (inset photo)

Front wall frame

Door

SHEDS

If your house has a yard, you can use a shed. It is that simple. Garages are for cars, basements are for household storage and laundries. But a shed is for tools that you need to keep your yard in good repair. Lawn mowers and tractors, rakes and shovels, bags of fertilizer or peat moss, tillers, chainsaws. . . The beauty of the shed is that you can fill it with just about anything, and it will be there waiting for you when you need it. Built from a kit or from scratch, a shed keeps your tools right where the action is.

KIT-BUILT SHED

For ease of installation and economy, the kit-built shed is a popular solution to back-yard storage problems. The wood-paneled, 10 × 12-ft. shed shown here goes together in much the same way as any other kit-built shed.

A shed kit typically includes the wall framing members and sheathing, door, roof frame, roof sheathing, trim and hardware, including fasteners. You can usually order a prefab plywood floor platform. You'll need to provide paint and the roof covering materials.

Kit-built Shed: A Six-step overview

1 Prepare the site (126 to 129)
2 Pour the slab (129 to 132)
3 Build the walls (133 to 137)
4 Frame & deck the roof (138 to 141)
5 Shingle the roof (141 to 143)
6 Finishing touches (143 to 144)

Photo 1:1 Mark the rough layout area (indicated by the small flags above) then use batterboards and mason's string to pinpoint the exact positions of the corners. Check to make sure the layout is exactly square. The 3-4-5 method is being used here: measure out 3 ft. and 4 ft. on the strings that form one corner and mark the points with tape. Measure the distance between the points. If the distance is 5 ft., then the corner is square. Check at all four corners.

Photo 1:2 After the layout is squared and you've checked to make sure the dimensions are correct, level the layout lines. Attach a line level to one of the strings and adjust the batterboards it is tied to until the string is level (you can do this by raising or lowering the crosspieces on the batter boards or by simply adjusting the height of the stakes that support the crosspieces).

If you've ever compared the price of building outdoor structures from scratch to buying a kit, you may have been surprised. While it seems logical that the kits would cost more (after all, much of the work has already been done), that often is not the case. Whether you're pricing playsets or fences or sheds, kits frequently are less costly. So you may ask yourself, "How do they do that?" Well, does it matter how? The real point is that if time and money are issues for you, it's hard to go wrong by buying a shed kit. And because you do have to construct a foundation, assemble all the parts and shingle the roof, you'll still get to experience the satisfaction of doing it yourself.

The 10 × 12-ft. shed kit we bought and assembled is made by *Handy Home Products* of Warren, Michigan. It features a gambrel roof and is clad in *T1-11* plywood. Plywood floor platform kits are available, but because the primary use for this shed is to house a lawn tractor, a more durable concrete floor was a better choice.

Regardless of how excited you might be about setting up your new shed kit, you need to do some planning and site preparation work before you bust open the kit. Your first stop should be the local building department. In fact, you might want to check into building requirements even before you buy the kit. Though it is unlikely, you don't want to get stuck with a kit that local building regulations prevent you from

assembling. Explain your plans and find out if any rules govern or restrict your work. Will you need a building permit (most sheds will). Are there setback requirements? Are on-site inspections required? These are the kinds of questions to ask before you begin.

Before you being preparing the construction site, make a call to your local public utility companies to have them check the property for buried lines or pipes (See Page 8).

Building regulations and utilities both can impact your site selection. Access is another key element. It may well be that the number of possible locations for the shed are very limited in your small yard. But for someone with a spacious yard (or with limited street access), the location of the shed can create a lot of extra hauling work. Ask yourself: "Will I need to cart gravel and concrete a considerable distance? Will I be able to have the shed package dropped right beside the slab? Will I have to carry every stick and nail from one end of your property to the other?" If you answer "Yes," you may want to investigate other site options.

ONE: Prepare the site

For small structures like this shed, a plain 4-in.-thick concrete slab makes an excellent foundation. In most cases, you can simply strip away the vegetation and topsoil, and cast the slab in forms set up directly on the undisturbed subsoil. Where drainage is sub-par, you'll need to excavate deeper, add drainage rocks/gravel, compact the fill, then cast the slab on top of that.

Lay out the slab. A formed concrete slab is laid out much like any other square work area: by driving stakes and batterboards and connecting them with masons' strings. Once the strings are in position and leveled, you adjust them up and down and side to side as needed to assess the grade of the site and mark out the exact corners of the forms.

Lay out the perimeter of the slab with batterboards and masons' string, remembering to include the thickness of your form boards (add 3 in. to both dimensions—a 10 × 12 slab like the one shown here will have a layout area of 123 × 147 in.). For this slab, you can begin with either the length or the width. Just make sure the strings delineating the sides are parallel and the stakes that support the batterboards are planted at least 2 ft. outside the project area. Then, lay out the perpendicular sides, again with the stakes planted a couple of feet beyond the edge of the slab. The points at which strings cross will show the actual corners of the slab plus forms. Check to confirm that the corners form right angles. We used the *3-4-5 method (See Photo 1:1)* to check our layout for square.

Once you've established a square layout, level the strings so you can use them as a guide for excavating for the pour *(See Photo 1:2).* Slip a line level onto one of the strings and adjust the height of the batterboard to bring the string to level (you can do this either by raising or lowering the stakes, or by detaching the batterboard crosspiece and reattaching it at a higher or lower position). Adjust the other strings, using the line level, so they are at the same height as the leveled string. Once the strings are squared and leveled, mark the positions of the strings on the batter boards so you can remove and re-tie them without having to go through the whole procedure again.

Excavate and prepare the base for the slab. A firm, well drained subbase is critical to a long-lasting slab. Serious cracks and settling usually can be traced to a poor subbase. In most cases, undisturbed soil supports a concrete slab best. If you must use fill—to provide enhanced drainage under the slab, for example—be sure to compact it well. Small areas can be compacted with a hand tamper or a heavy lawn roller. If you need to use gravel fill over the entire site, rent a compactor.

To begin the excavation, remove sod, weeds, roots and any other organic matter from the site so you're down to bare dirt *(See Photo 1:3).* If the turf is in good shape and you need fresh sod, use a sod stripper (See page 11). To create access for the forms, excavate to 1 ft. beyond the perimeter of the area to be formed (this

Photo 1:3 Remove all sod and loose debris from the work area so you can accurately assess the grade and the soil condition. Clear the ground at least 1 ft. outside each layout line.

Photo 1:4 Make a story pole marked to indicate the distance of the highest point of the site from the level lines. Then mark off the excavation depth above this line and use the story pole as a guide for excavating to an even depth.

Photo 1:5 Compact the soil in the worksite with a plate vibrator or hand tamper, especially if you have filled in with any new subbase material.

Photo 1:6 Drive stakes around the perimeter of the construction area to support the form boards. When laying out the area, add 3 in. to each direction to allow for the thickness of the form boards.

is the main reason the batterboards are installed well outside the work area). To determine the required depth of the excavation, add the thickness of the slab (4 in., in this case) to the thickness of the subbase, if needed (also 4 in.). Subtract 1 in. (the approximate amount the slab should project above grade). Make a story pole to quickly measure this distance at the layout strings (you'll need to figure in the distance of the strings above the highest grade point, of course). Excavate to the required depth, checking periodically with the story pole *(See Photo 1:4).*

Photo 1:7 Attach the form boards (2 × 4s are used most often) to the stakes with deck screws. Screws can be backed out easily when it's time to break the forms.

When the excavation is finished, check for soft or mucky spots. If you find any, they should be dug out and filled with sand or gravel. Then, add subbase fill if needed. The best subbase is compactible gravel (sometimes called Class V or Class II). Dump a load of fill into the work area and compact it until it's 4 in. thick. We didn't add subbase, but we compacted the soil with a plate vibrator anyway *(See Photo 1:5).*

Construct the forms. To build concrete slab forms, most people use 2 × 4 (they're only 3½ in. wide, but enough of the concrete will settle into the subbase that the slab will be close enough to 4 in. thick after the pour). The form boards need to be braced with wooden stakes—usually 1 × 2 or 2 × 2. Begin setting up your forms by driving stakes into the ground, spacing them about 2 or 3 ft. apart. Line up each stake so its inside face touches the layout string *(See Photo 1:6)*. You may need to use a level to extend the plane of the stake up to reach the layout string. Pound in the stakes so the tops are slightly less than 3½ in. above ground (if they're higher than the form boards you won't be able to tool the concrete). All stakes must be driven straight and true if forms are to be plumb.

Cut the form boards to length (if you use more than one board to make any of the runs, make sure the seam between boards is reinforced with a stake directly behind it). Position the form boards inside the stakes and attach them by driving screws through the stakes and into the forms—avoid driving all the way through the forms. Also screw through the ends of the form boards and into the mating form boards to reinforce the corners. Check to make sure all the form boards are plumb and aligned with the layout strings. Now you can remove the layout strings.

TWO: Pour the slab

Preparing. Make sure to order enough concrete—coming up short can be disastrous. For the 10 × 12-ft. slab shown here, we only needed 1½ yards, but we ordered two full yards to allow for waste and just to be safe. Before the truck arrives with your concrete, a few pieces of information should be marked on the form boards. One is locations for the J-bolts that are installed in the fresh concrete to secure the shed sills to the slab. Typically, the J-bolts are positioned about 4 ft. apart. We planned to embed three ½-in.-dia. × 5-in.-long J-bolts about 3 in. deep into the edge of the slab, spacing three along each side and the back, and two near the corners along the front. The resulting 2-in. projection of threaded bolt is about right for securing 2 × 4 sills.

The second marking is for con-

Photo 2:1 Begin placing the concrete at the corner of the work site furthest from the access point. Try to get the concrete as close to the correct thickness when you unload it to minimize the need to move the material around. Begin striking off with a screed as soon as you can. Make sure to have plenty of help on hand for the pour.

trol joints, if you choose to cut them in the slab (See *Controlling Cracks,* page 131). On this project, it just happened that the control joints would fall on the centerlines of the sides, which also were locations of J-bolts.

The day the concrete is to be delivered, be sure you have the tools you need at the job site. Basic items needed for a typical job include at least one wheelbarrow (preferably two or three, with eager pushers), a shovel, a long straightedge (usually a 2 × 4) for screeding the concrete, a bull float or darby, an edger, a groover for cutting the control joints, a float, a trowel, and a ready water supply.

There is no getting around one basic fact of pouring a concrete slab: you will need help when the truck arrives. The deliveryman will discharge the concrete directly into the forms if he can get the truck close to the job site. He will not push a wheelbarrow for you. If concrete can be discharged directly

from the truck into the forms, usually with a chute, you still will need one or two helpers to strike and finish it before it cures.

Just before the concrete is scheduled to arrive, dampen the subbase—this is especially important in hot weather, to keep the dry subbase from sucking water out of the concrete and causing weakening during the cure. Likewise, wooden forms should be hosed down. To make breaking the forms easier, coat the insides with vegetable oil. Set the reinforcing steel (re-bar or re-wire) in place if you are going to use one of these products instead of cutting control joints—in a slab of this size you can go either way (See page 131).

Placing. When the truck arrives, have a clear path laid out between the delivery area and the site. Also, construct a ramp so you can get your wheelbarrows up and over the form boards. Begin loading your wheelbarrows then dumping them in the formed area *(See Photo 2:1)*.

Photo 2:2 Use a straight 2 × 4 (a 12-footer is shown here) to strike off the concrete so it is level with the tops of the form. Make sure there are no ridges or dips. Move the screed board in a back-and-forth sawing motion.

Photo 2:3 Smooth the concrete surface with a bull float (a rental item). When pushing the bull float, tip the leading edge up slightly so it doesn't dig in.

Photo 2:4 On the pull stroke, raise the back edge of the bull float slightly. Float the concrete until the surface is smooth and even, but avoid overworking it.

Concrete should not be dumped in piles, then dragged out with a rake or hoe. Doing this will tend to separate the ingredients, because mortar (the sand and cement) tends to flow ahead of coarse aggregate. Too much water and fine material rise to the surface, and this can cause scaling and dusting of the cured surface. Instead, start in the far corner from the entry ramp and place the concrete in even rows that are roughly the thickness of the planned slab. This entails backing up with the wheelbarrow as you unload it, so it's important not to overfill the wheelbarrow to the point that you can't control it. With a shovel, fill in with concrete at the edges of the forms and move it around as needed for even coverage. Work the nose of the shovel between the form and the concrete to settle out voids. But do take care not to overwork the material.

Tooling. You should begin screeding (also called "striking off") the concrete before all the concrete is placed. Use a straight 2 × 4 (we used a 12-footer) as a screed. Rest the 2 × 4 on top of the forms. The object is to skim off the excess concrete in a sawing motion so the surface is flush to or just slightly higher than the top of the form *(See Photo 2:2).*

When all the concrete is placed and screeded, smooth it with a bullfloat or a darby (both tools can be rented). A bullfloat has a long handle and is used to smooth areas too large to reach with a darby. Work the bullfloat as you would a sponge mop. As you push the tool away from yourself, tip the front up so it will compact the concrete without digging in *(See Photo 2:3).* As you pull the bullfloat back toward yourself, run it flat on the concrete to cut off bumps and fill holes *(See Photo 2:4).* The darby is short and low-handled, giving you more control in the easy to reach areas. It is moved across the concrete in a sawing motion. After smoothing, cut the top inch or so of the concrete away from the forms using a pointed trowel.

As soon as the floating is completed, push the J-bolts into the concrete. The bolts should be positioned at the spots you marked on the forms, set about 1¼ in. from the inside edge of the form board. As the concrete sets up, slice it away from the forms with a mason's (bricklayer's) trowel *(See Photo 2:5)*.

Monitor the concrete as it cures. When water rises to the surface of the concrete, then evaporates, it is time to edge the concrete and cut control joints. Run the edging tool along an edge (choose a less visible spot). If the concrete holds the rounded shape of the metal edging tool, finish the first edging operation, applying with firm, steady

Photo 2:5 Slice the concrete along the edges of the form as it begins to set up, using a trowel. This creates a smoother edge and makes the form boards easier to release.

Photo 2:6 Once the bleed water has disappeared from the concrete surface, tool the edges of the slab with an edging tool. You should probably wear gloves when performing this job.

CONTROLLING CRACKS

Concrete is constantly expanding and contracting, which causes stress and, inevitably, cracks. You can't prevent the cracking, but you can control it. Two techniques are used to control cracking. One is the use of steel reinforcement (rebar and rewire), which serves purposes beyond crack control. For smaller slabs like the one shown here, reinforcement is not required. So we chose the other option: cutting "control joints."

Control joints encourage the concrete to crack in straight lines and at planned locations. We cut one control joint along the centerline of the slab. A control joint should cut about one-quarter of the way through the slab. Slabs wider than about 10 to 12 ft. should have more than one control joint, including a longitudinal control joint down the center. If possible, the panels formed by

Option 1: Cut control joints with a groover after the concrete has stiffened, but before it has hardened.

Option 2: Cut control joints with a circular saw and masonry blade after the concrete has set up.

control joints should be approximately square. All control joints should be placed as continuous (not staggered or offset) lines. Cut

them with a groover while the concrete is fresh, or with a circular saw and masonry blade after the concrete has set.

pressure *(See Photo 2:6)*. Tip the tool up slightly as you work, so it doesn't dig into the concrete. And don't press down too hard. Gouges and depressions created by the various finishing tools are difficult to remove at this stage. (edging the slab for the shed is not as critical as it is when you're pouring a sidewalk or patio with exposed edges.)

Control joints (See Controlling Cracks, previous page). The next step is adding the control joints. Use a board at least 6 in. wide as a straightedge to guide the jointing tool and to kneel on as you work. It's a lot easier to do the job if you use a 2 × 12, which will give you a lot more space for kneeling. Before cutting the control joints, snap a chalk line across the slab to mark the line of the joint. Lay the 2 × 12 across the forms, parallel to the chalk line. Press the groover firmly into the concrete and guide it along the 2 × 12 as you cut the joint. Keep the nose of the tool slightly elevated. After you've moved all the way across the slab and roughed out the joint, turn around and slide the tool back through the groove, smoothing and finishing it.

Floating usually is the last step in finishing outdoor concrete. Use a wooden or metal hand float to further smooth the surface. Work the float flat on the concrete, in wide, arc motions. But don't press too hard. It is hard to erase gouges made at this point.

NOTE: Sometimes concrete is troweled to make it even smoother and more dense on the surface. But this extra smoothness isn't desirable inside the shed, because it can be slippery when wet. An alternative is to trowel the concrete, then scarify the surface with a stiff-bristled brush after the last troweling. The first troweling is done immediately after floating. If you need to kneel on a board to reach areas, you can float an area and then trowel it before moving the board. Hold the trowel flat against the concrete. The second troweling should be done later, when your hand leaves only a slight impression in the concrete.

Curing. Keep the concrete damp while it cures. It takes about a month for typical concrete to cure to its full strength. The first 5 to 7 days, depending on the weather, are the most crucial. During this time, you must make sure the concrete has a chance to cure slowly by keeping it moist. Cover it with plastic sheeting, damp burlap or straw and sprinkle it periodically. The forms can be removed after several days. For best results, allow a few extra days of curing time before using the surface.

Photo 2:7 Proper curing is critical to the durability of your new concrete slab. If the concrete dries too quickly it will be subject to a number of possible defects, including spalling (flaking off of the surface) and cracking. For a full week after the pour, keep the slab covered with a plastic tarp. Once or twice a day you should dampen the surface with water, then recover it. Dampen it even more frequently in hot weather.

Photo 3:1 Set the sill boards in position lengthwise on the slab and use a square to mark a refence line aligned with the center of each J-bolt onto the tops of the sills.

Photo 3:2 Measure the distance from the center of each J-bolt to the edge of the slab, then measure along the sill reference line that same distance and mark a drilling centerpoint.

THREE: Build the walls

After the slab has been cast and has cured for a good week, you can erect the shed, starting with the walls. Even if you don't build a *Handy Homes* model similar to the one shown here, you can be confident that yours will go together in much the same way. Study the directions supplied with the shed, and follow them to the letter.

Drill guide holes for the J-bolts. Cut the sills to length from pressure-treated 2 × 4 stock (some shed kits will not include sill plates because the kits are meant to work on a variety of foundations, including plywood platforms, where sill plates may not be required). The side sills are just under 12 ft. long. The end sill is 10 ft. long. The two front sills, located on either side of the doorway, are 28 in. long. Lay each sill on the slab and set it against the J-bolts. Transfer the J-bolt locations to the sills using a square—we used a combination square *(See Photo 3:1).* Measure the distance of the middle of each J-bolt from the edge of the slab, then use this measurement to mark a drilling point for the guide hole in the sill, at the reference line *(See Photo 3:2).* Drill holes and check the fit, but don't bolt the sills in place yet.

Inventory the parts. The paperwork packed with the shed skit should include a list of all the parts. Now's the time to make sure you have everything you need. Spread the parts out and collect each subassembly's components in one spot. This will help you get a sense of what's involved in the work ahead, it will organize the parts so you can work efficiently, and it will reveal

Photo 3:3 Using the slab as a worksurface, begin constructing the walls of the shed. Start by screwing the back wall components together with 3-in. deck screws.

Photo 3:4 Attach the precut wall sheathing panels to the wall frames with 2-in. siding nails. Follow the manufacturer's directions carefully when assembling the walls, paying special attention to the overhang and setback amounts for the sheathing panels.

Photo 3:5 Erect the walls one at a time, beginning with the back wall. Set the guide holes you drilled in the sill over the J-bolts, level and plumb the wall, then attach a staked brace or two to hold the wall in position temporarily.

anything that's missing (See Photo, page 124). If something is missing, you can, of course, call and have a part sent. But you may find it more convenient to make the part.

Construct the back wall. Move the frame members for the back wall—the sill, the extension wall braces, and the center wall supports—onto the slab. Join the two center wall supports with the precut cross-lap joint. Butt the extension wall braces against the ends of the horizontal element of the center-wall support unit next. Drive 3 in. deck screws through the braces into the ends of the support *(See Photo 3:3).*

Butt the sill against the ends of the braces and the vertical support. The middle of the sill (60 in. from each end) should line up on the centerline of the vertical support. Marke sure all the vertical elements are perpendicular to the sill (measure diagonally from brace to brace to check this; the diagonal measurements should be equal). Screw through the bottom face of the sill into the ends of the three vertical frame members.

Set the two large wall panels in place on the framework. They should butt edge-to-edge over the center of the center support, and their bottom edges should overhang the top of the sill by ½ in. Nail them to the frame members with 2-in. siding nails, spacing the nails about 8 in. apart *(See Photo 3:4).* Place and nail the wing panels next. You'll need to slip 2 × 3s under the outside edges of these wings to support them. Nail the wings to the wall frame members.

Erect the back wall. Erecting the back wall is a simple matter of lifting it onto the J-bolts, making sure it is level and plumb, then temporarily attaching a 2 × 4 brace to the outside of the wall. Stake the brace to the ground to hold the wall in place until the other walls are installed to support it *(See*

Photo 3:5). If it is necessary to plumb the back wall, slip cedar shims between the wing panels and the end studs. Then, tighten washers and nuts onto the threaded J-bolts sticking up through the sill *(See Photo 3:6).*

Construct the side walls. The side walls are conventional stud walls, and they can be constructed and erected just like conventional stud walls. The sills on the side-walls should be shorted by 3½ in. each to provide clearance for the front and back wall sills. For the same reason, the end studs should be cut 1½ in. short at the bottoms. Lay out the sill and the top plate, and arrange the studs between them. The studs are located 24 in. on-center (except for one of the end studs, which is 20⅝ in. from the adjacent stud). When the layout is set, drive 3-in. screws through the sill and the top plate and into the ends of the studs.

Make sure the frame is square (measure the diagonals), then lay the side wall panels over it. Align the top edges of the panels flush with the top plate. The ends of the panel should be flush with the end studs. The bottom edges should overhang the top of the sill by ½ in. Drive 2-in. siding nails through the panels into the plate, studs and sill *(See Photo 3:7).* Build both side walls, but do not erect them yet.

Construct the front wall. Because it contains the door opening, the front wall is the trickiest to construct. Position the right front wall panel on a flat surface (the week-old concrete slab is an excellent work area). The door should be facing up. Lift the panel enough to slide the center front wall support under the panel above the door, edge up. The panel should, of course, be lined up on the center-line of the support. Lift the other edge of the panel and slide the extension-wall brace under the panel, aligning its centerline with

Photo 3:6 After level and plumb are established, secure the walls by threading washers and nuts over the J-bolts and tightening the nuts with a socket wrench. Get them good and snug, but take care not to overtighten the nuts.

Photo 3:7 Construct the short sidewall frame by driving 3-in. deck screws through the sill and top plate and into the ends of the studs. The ends of the sill are cut short to allow for the width of the front and back wall sills.

Photo 3:8 Attach the sheathing panels to the sidewalls with 2-in. siding nails spaced at 8-in. intervals. Set the completed sidewalls out of the way until after both the back wall and front wall are set up.

3:9

Photo 3:9 Construct the front wall with the framing members slipped in beneath the sheathing panels. Because of the door and framed door opening, the front wall is usually the trickiest of the four to put together, so take your time.

3:10

Temporary battens

Photo 3:10 Cut some temporary battens (we used the waferboard packing material from the shed kit) and screw them across the door seams to keep the door shut securely when the wall is erected. Finish up the construction of the front wall by screwing up through the sill and into the bottom ends of the wall studs.

the panel's edge. The bottom end of the extension-wall brace should be aligned 2½ in. from the bottom edge of the wall panel. Additional support for the wall panel can be provided temporarily by sliding a piece of 2 × 3 stock under the door.

With the panel well supported, drive 2-in. siding nails through the edge of the wall panel into the front wall support and the wall-extension brace. Space the nails approximately 8 in. apart. (Don't drive any nails into the temporary support, of course.)

Place the wing-panel on the extension-wall brace. Use a length of 2 × 3, set on edge, under the wing panel as a temporary support while you align and nail the wing to the brace.

Bring the left front wall panel into position next. The door will be supported by the temporary support you still have under the right-hand door. The section above the door must rest on the front wall support, and the outer edge should rest on an extension-wall brace. Position this brace 2½ in. from the bottom edge of the wall panel, as you did on the right side. Place the two ⅜-in.-thick door spacers between the latch-edges of the two doors, and make sure the two wall sections are aligned properly.

Nail through the left wall panel into the front wall support and the extension-wall brace *(See Photo 3:9)*. Use 2-in. nails and space them approximately 8 in. apart. At the gable peak, toe-nail through the trim on the right panel into the trim on the left panel. Position the left wing panel, in the same fashion that you did the right wing panel, and nail it to the assembly.

Screw the trim to the wall panels above the door next. After the wall is erected, you will permanently attach this trim by driving fasteners from inside the shed. But this trim will help hold the wall components together while you set it up, so for now, drive four screws through the trim into the wall panels.

Secure the doors with temporary battens by scabbing two pieces of the waferboard packing material across the joint between the doors *(See Photo 3:10)*. Align one at the bottom, and drive three screws through each batten and into each door. Position the piece at the top so it laps over the top trim you just installed. Screw this piece to the doors and the trim.

Finally, screw the sills to the bottom ends of the extension-wall braces, then nail the wall panels to the sills. Each sill should extend ⅛ in. past the edge of the front wall assembly. (The assembly should measure 119¾ in. across the bottom, while the outside ends of the sills should be 120 in. apart.)

Erect the front wall. Before erecting the front wall, cut a brace like the one you used for the rear wall and have it ready.

Stand the wall upright, slide it into alignment with the J-bolts, then lift it and drop it over the bolts. Get the wall roughly plumbed, and screw the brace to the wall. Drive a stake into the ground beside the far end of the brace. Square up the wall again so it's perfectly plumb then screw the brace to the stake. The last job is to slip a washer over each J-bolt, then thread the nut onto it. Tighten the nut.

Before erecting the sidewalls, open the doors in the front wall. Back out the screws in the battens that are keeping the doors closed. When the doors are open, permanently attach the trim above them by driving screws through the interior side of the wall panels into the trim boards.

Erect the sidewalls. Set one of the sidewalls onto the J-bolts *(See Photo 3:11)*. The end studs of the sidewall should rest on the ends of the front and back sills. Be careful

3:11

Photo 3:11 Position the sidewalls over their J-bolts, making sure they're flush with the sides of the front and back walls. Attach washers and nuts to the J-bolts. Note: Unless you're a world-class hurdler, it's wise to remove the temporary battens from the door before installing the sidewalls so you don't get trapped inside the shed.

not to disturb the front and back walls. Plumb the side wall at the front, and drive nails through the front wall into the adjacent sidewall studs, tying the two together *(See Photo 3:12)*. Install the washers and nuts on the J-bolts, and tighten the side wall against the concrete slab.

Construct and erect the second side wall in the same way.

Install the trim. Attach the "weatherstrip" to the inside of the door on the right side (viewed from inside the shed), so the strip covers the gap between the two doors. Use the 1¼-in. screws provided, locating them about 8 in. apart.

Step outside the shed, close both doors, and mount the hasp and staple. The staple is mounted on the left door, the hasp on the right. You want to install them so that the hasp, when closed onto the staple, covers the mounting screws for both pieces.

Install the rest of the trim. This includes the soffit end caps, the front and back wall trim, and the corner trim *(See Photo 3:13)*.

Photo 3:12 Drive siding nails through the sides of the front and back wall panels and into the end studs of the sidewalls to complete the basic wall structure of the shed.

Photo 3:13 Attach the trim boards before proceeding with the roof installation. The trim kit includes the top trim pieces for the front wall, corner trim, and the soffit end caps being installed in this photo.

TRACTOR SHED Step Four: Build the roof

FOUR: Frame & deck the roof

Assemble the trusses. The trusses are delivered in halves. You must join two halves with a pair of gussets to form a complete truss unit.

First, measure across the side wall plates. Hook your tape over the outside of one side wall and measure across to the outside of the other wall. Subtract 1 in. for the thickness of the side wall panels. This measurement is how far apart the ends of the trusses must be when they are assembled.

Lay out a pair of the truss halves. Butt the upper ends together. Spread the bottom ends apart to the necessary measurement. Nail or screw one of the the gussets to the faces of the truss halves, linking the halves together *(See Photo 4:1).* Turn the truss over and attach the second gusset. Repeat this assembly process until all five trusses are assembled.

Set up the trusses. The trusses stand on the side-wall plates. In the *Handy Home* line, the trusses are

always set on 2-ft. centers, but the base point for the layout varies according to the shed size. For our 10 × 12-ft. shed, the base point is the center truss (of five). It's back face is positioned 70 5/16 in. from the inside of the front wall. The other trusses are placed 2-ft. on-center, measured from the center truss.

Rather than struggle to align each truss with a tape measure, measure and mark the locations for them on the plates. Then simply lift each truss into place, align it with its marks, and toenail it to the plate with 16d common nails *(See Photo 4:2).*

Build the soffits. The soffits are built onto the shed at the tops of the side walls and project out from the side. Rainwater shed by the roof won't run directly down the walls, thanks to the soffits. This will prolong the life of the shed.

You've already installed the soffit end caps. Now you must mount the soffit nailers. One nailer is attached to the wall at the end of each truss. Because

Photo 4:1 The roof trusses arrive in two sections that must be joined together with gussets at the top. Attach a gusset to each side of each truss assembly. Make all the roof trusses.

Photo 4:2 Set the trusses in position, beginning with the center truss. Toenail the trusses to the top wall plates with 16d common nails.

in the 10 × 12-ft. shed the trusses are positioned just off the wall studs, mounting the soffit nailers is relatively easy. Hold the nailer in place against the sidewall, ¼ in. below the wall's top edge. From inside the shed, drive a couple of screws through the wall into the ends of the nailers *(See Photo 4:3)*.

With the nailers mounted, install the fascia next. This trim piece fits into the rabbets in the ends of the soffit caps. Drive finish nails through the end caps into the ends of the fascia, then nail through the fascia into the ends of the nailers.

The soffit roof panels go on next. Two panels are used on each side of the shed. Set each panel in position and nail it to the end cap and the nailers. We used a pneumatic nailer for this job *(See Photo 4:4)*, but a plain old hammer will do just as well.

Sheathe the roof. All the panels used in sheathing the roof are pre-

cut. Installing them is a simple matter of setting them into place, one at a time, and nailing them to the trusses and the edges of the front and back walls. As you do this, it is important to keep the trusses from shifting out of correct position.

Start with the lower roof sections. Set the large panel in place, with one end aligned on the centerline of the fourth truss from the back and the other end held ³⁄₁₆ in. back from the face of the back wall trim. Nail it to the shed only at its corners for now, in case you must adjust the position or trim the panel to get the correct fit of both lower roof panels on that side. Position the smaller panel next. It should butt tightly against the large panel over the truss and be back ³⁄₁₆ in. from the face of the trim. Nail it at the corners.

If both panels fit correctly—the setback from the trim is critical—

then nail the panels to the roof trusses and the edges of the front and back walls. Use the same 8-in. spacing you've used everywhere else. The first nails you drive should be close to the upper edges of the panels, and before driving one of these nails, double-check the truss spacing to ensure that none of the trusses shifted or distorted slightly as you placed the panels *(See Photo 4:5)*. Once you have a nail through the panels into each truss, you can finish nailing. Install the two lower panels on the other side of the roof.

Position the panels on the upper roof next. Here, you want to reverse the positions of the large and small panels, and you need to shift the setbacks as well. At the front of the shed, the edges of the roof panels should be set back ³⁄₈ in. At the back, the panel edges should be flush with the wall trim. The panels need to be tight at the

Photo 4:3 Attach soffit nailers to the sidewalls by driving screws through the wall panels and into the inside edges of the nailers.

Photo 4:4 After attaching the soffit fascia boards, nail the soffit sheathing panels to the soffit nailers.

Photo 4:5 Install the lower roof panels on each side of the roof. Tack them at the corners first in case you need to trim them slightly. Once they fit, nail them to the trusses.

Photo 4:6 Install the roof sheathing on the upper roof sections.

Photo 4:7 Construct the two gable overhang sections, then attach them to the front wall trim boards.

roof peak, which will leave a slight gap between the panels of the lower and upper roofs.

Place a panel and nail its corners. When all four panels are in place, nail them to the trusses and wall trim *(See Photo 4:6)*.

Install the gable overhang. There should be four parts left: the parts that make up the gable overhang. Two are triangular pieces of the roof sheathing material, while the others are 2 × 3 supports. Lay one of the roof pieces atop the appropriate support and nail it in place. Assemble the second half of the overhang in the same way.

To install the overhang, set the edge of one of the units on top of the front wall, back against the edge of the roof panel. Drive nails down through the triangular roof piece into the wall trim. Drive a couple of nails through the support into the trim as well.

Attach the second piece in the same way .*(See Photo 4:7)*. Then, toenail though one triangular roof piece into the adjacent unit's support. Toenail in the opposite direction as well.

FIVE: Shingle the roof

Materials required for actually weatherproofing the roof are not included in the kit. For the 10 × 12 shed we built, we needed to buy seven bundles of shingles, drip edge molding and building paper.

Cut and install the drip edge molding on the bottom edges of the sheathing. Any joints between individual strips should be positioned somewhere other than a corner. The end of one strip should overlap the its neighbor by about 1 in.

With the drip edge nailed in place, apply building paper (we used 15-pound). This can be cut into strips as necessary and stretched out in horizontal courses beginning at the bottom edge *(See Photo 5:1)*. You want the building paper to overlay the seams

Photo 5:1 Attach drip-edge molding along the bottom edges of the soffit sheathing, then apply 15-pound building paper over the roof. Start stapling the building paper at the low end of each roof side. After the building paper is installed, attach drip edge to the side edges of the sheathing.

Photo 5:2 Install the starter course of shingles upside down. Use the lines printed on the building paper for reference.

between sheathing panels to forestall leaks. The first course should overlap the drip edge, and the second and third courses as you work toward the peak should each overlay the previous course.

Install drip edge at the side edges of the roof, overlapping the building paper. At the corners, the drip-edge should follow around. The proper approach here is to cut wedges out of the flange that overlays the sheathing so you can bend the material to follow the roof-edge contour.

Start shingling the roof at the bottom edges on each side of the shed. Peel the cellophane strip off the back of each shingle before you apply it. Align the first course of shingles across the soffit projection, orienting the edge with the slots facing up the roof slope. Nail the shingles in place with roofing nails *(See Photo 5:2)*, positioning them along the line marked across the center of the shingle.

Apply the second course directly over the first course, orienting the edges of the shingles with the

Photo 5:3 Work your way up toward the ridge when installing the shingles. Be sure to stagger the shingle tabs so they are not aligned.

Photo 5:4 Shingle up over the ridge from each direction. Trim the overhanging shingles with a utility knife or aviator snips.

Photo 5:5 Cut and trim the shingle tabs from whole shingles and use them for the ridge cap shingles. Start nailing at one end—generally, the end that's less exposed to the prevailing wind direction.

Photo 5:6 Since the last ridge cap shingle will not be overlapped by another to cover the nail heads, apply plastic roof cement to the nails heads to seal the nail holes.

slots down *(See Photo 5:3)*. All subsequent courses are oriented tab-edge down, and must overlap the preceding course by half the width of the shingle. The slots should be staggered from course to course. To keep the courses straight, follow the lines printed on the paper. Shingle both sides all the way up and over the peak *(See Photo 5:4)*, making sure the final course on each side has enough "good" surface to cover.

At the peak of the roof, install "ridge caps" to seal the seam. To make a ridge cap, cut a shingle into thirds and trim off the top corners of the tab (non-mineralized) at a 30° angle. Starting at the back of the shed, fold a ridge cap across the ridge and nail it in place. Follow that with another ridge cap, then another *(See Photo 5:5)*. Work your way along the ridge to the front of the shed. The last cap is made from a one-third shingle that's had the un-mineralized material cut off. The roofing nails used to fasten this cap will be exposed. Cover each nail head with roofing cement *(See Photo 5:6)*.

SIX: Finishing touches

If you haven't done it already, mount the barrel bolt to the side of the door containing the weatherstripping. The bolt should be attached to the door and the catch to the gable wall. The assembly should be positioned close to the weatherstrip. Also attach the four door stiffeners *(See Photo 6:1)*. These turnbuckles are used to adjust the door alignment and to keep the door panels from warping.

Paint the shed. Don't delay in priming and painting the shed. Paint will significantly improve the life of your shed by deterring damage caused by the sun's ultra-violet radiation and by moisture. The design of the trim suggests that you use a two-color paint job, although obviously that is a bit more work.

Photo 6:1 Attach any remaining hardware, including the metal stiffeners that are attached to the inside of the door panels. The stiffeners are essentially turn-buckles that can be adjusted to bring the doors into alignment in the door frames.

Photo 6:2 Prime the entire shed. Because we planned to use a relatively light-colored paint, we chose a white, stain-killing primer product.

Photo 6:3 Paint the shed. Typically, the shed is painted in the same color scheme as your house (some neighborhood covenants require that outbuildings be the same color as the main structure). If you are painting the trim a contrasting color, paint the walls first, then mask the walls and paint the trim.

But suit yourself. Begin the job by caulking all the seams with good-quality caulk. Hit all the seams between walls and trim and between the wall panels on the front and back.

Prime the whole shed—trim, wall panels, and doors *(See Photo 6:2)*. Either latex or oil-based primer can be used. You may hear a lot of opinions about which type of primer and/or paint is better. Some will recommend priming with latex then top-coating with oil-based paint. Others will recommend doing it the other way around—latex paint over an oil-based primer. However, most coatings specialists will tell you that latex coating keeps getting better, and that using latex paint over a latex primer will give you the longest-lasting coating. Moreover, the job will get done more quickly (because latex dries faster) and clean-up will be easier.

Primer typically is white, but it can be difficult to conceal it under a single top-coat of a dark color. You can save yourself some work and some paint if you have the primer tinted. You don't necessarily have to match the paint color; tinting it a medium gray is enough to make it easier to cover with a color.

Read the paint manufacturer's directions printed on the can. Prime the shed and allow it to dry as long as the manufacturer stipulates. Top-coat the shed with at least two coats of quality paint *(See Photo 6:3)*.

Build a driveway. To make it easier to get rolling equipment (in our case, a lawn tractor) in and out of the shed, we built a "driveway." We simply staked a pair of short pressure-treated 2 × 4s to the ground so their tops were level with the top of the slab at the shed end and at grade on the open end. We filled the space between the 2 × 4s with compactible gravel, then tamped it down with a hand tamper. *(See Photo 6:4).* For a decorative touch, we installed landscape edging from the front of the driveway back to the edges of the shed in a semicircular pattern, creating a pair of symmetrical planting beds.

Photo 6:4 Install a driveway feature and do a little landscaping to dress up your new shed and make it easier to use. We created a compactible gravel "driveway" set into a semicircular planting bed.

VENTILATION

Ventilation is a very important feature to include in your shed. The best way to go about it is simply to cut a vent hole or two at the top of your back wall. Cover the vent holes with louvered soffit vent covers. Make sure the covers are equipped with insect mesh.

Tool Shed

The basic tool shed is a must for any handyman or gardener. Building one is an unbeatable way to create practical storage for garden and lawn maintenance tools; and building it from scratch will help your tool shed stand out from the sameness of kit sheds and yard barns. The construction is simple, the price tag is low and building your own shed is a highly satisfying backyard project.

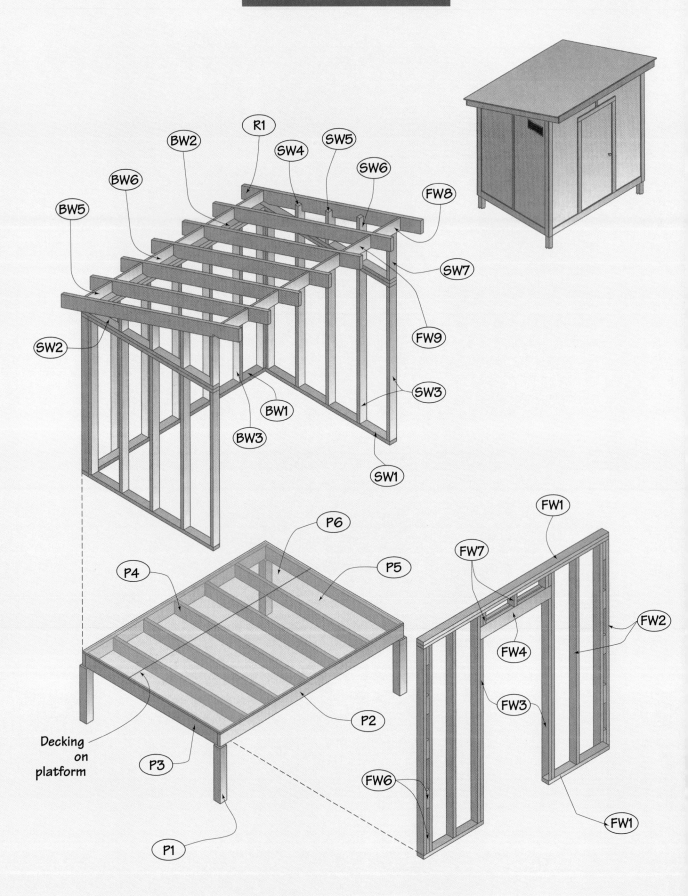

OVERALL DIMENSIONS (99"W × 103"L × 111¾"H)

KEY	PART NAME	QTY.	SIZE	MATERIAL
PLATFORM				
P1	POST	4	3½ × 3½ × 24"	PRESSURE TREATED
P2	RIM JOIST - FRONT/BACK	2	1½ × 5½ × 96"	DIMENSIONAL LUMBER (2x6)
P3	RIM JOIST - SIDE	2	1½ × 5½ × 69"	DIMENSIONAL LUMBER (2x6)
P4	FLOOR JOIST	5	1½ × 5½ × 69"	DIMENSIONAL LUMBER (2x6)
P5	FLOOR DECKING	1	¾ × 48 × 96"	CDX PLYWOOD
P6	FLOOR DECKING	1	¾ × 24 × 96"	CDX PLYWOOD
P7	EXT. SHEATHING - SIDE	2	¾ × 5¼ × 73½"	CDX PLYWOOD
P8	EXT. SHEATHING - FRONT/BACK	2	¾ × 5¼ × 96"	CDX PLYWOOD
BACK WALL				
BW1	SOLE/TOP PLATE	2	1½ × 3½ × 96"	DIMENSIONAL LUMBER (2x4)
BW2	CAP PLATE	1	1½ × 3½ × 89"	DIMENSIONAL LUMBER (2x4)
BW3	STUDS	9	1½ × 3½ × 67⅜"	DIMENSIONAL LUMBER (2x4)
BW4	CORNER BLOCKING	8	1½ × 3½ × 8"	DIMENSIONAL LUMBER (2x4)
BW5	RAFTER BLOCKING	2	¾ × 4⅝ × 13¾"	DIMENSIONAL LUMBER (1x6)
BW6	RAFTER BLOCKING	4	¾ × 4⅝ × 14½"	DIMENSIONAL LUMBER (1x6)
BW7	SHEATHING	2	¾ × 48 × 71½"	TEXTURED PLYWOOD
SIDE WALL (QUANTITY IS FOR TWO WALLS)				
SW1	SOLE/TOP PLATE	4	1½ × 3½ × 65"	DIMENSIONAL LUMBER (2x4)
SW2	CAP PLATE	2	1½ × 3½ × 68½"	DIMENSIONAL LUMBER (2x4)
SW3	STUDS	10	1½ × 3½ × 67⅜"	DIMENSIONAL LUMBER (2x4)
SW4	CRIPPLE	2	1½ × 3½ × "8 ⅞"	DIMENSIONAL LUMBER (2x4)
SW5	CRIPPLE	2	1½ × 3½ × 14¼"	DIMENSIONAL LUMBER (2x4)
SW6	CRIPPLE	2	1½ × 3½ × 19½"	DIMENSIONAL LUMBER (2x4)
SW7	CRIPPLE	2	1½ × 3½ × 24¾"	DIMENSIONAL LUMBER (2x4)
SW8	SHEATHING	2	¼ × 36¾ × 83¾"	TEXTURED PLYWOOD
SW9	SHEATHING	2	¾ × 36¾ × 96"	TEXTURED PLYWOOD
FRONT WALL				
FW1	SOLE/TOP PLATE	3	1½ × 3½ × 96"	DIMENSIONAL LUMBER (2x4)
FW2	STUDS	8	1½ × 3½ × 90¼"	DIMENSIONAL LUMBER (2x4)
FW3	TRIMMER STUDS	2	1½ × 3½ × 79½"	DIMENSIONAL LUMBER (2x4)
FW4	HEADER	2	1½ × 5½ × 37"	DIMENSIONAL LUMBER (2x6)
FW5	HEADER BLOCKING	1	½ × 5 × 37"	SCRAP PLYWOOD
FW6	CORNER BLOCKING	10	1½ × 3½ × 8"	DIMENSIONAL LUMBER (2x4)
FW7	CRIPPLES	5	1½ × 3½ × 5 ¼"	DIMENSIONAL LUMBER (2x4)
FW8	RAFTER BLOCKING	2	¾ × 5½ × 13 ¾"	DIMENSIONAL LUMBER (1x6)
FW9	RAFTER BLOCKING	4	¾ × 5½ × 14½"	DIMENSIONAL LUMBER (1x6)
FW10	SHEATHING	2	¾ × 48 × 96"	TEXTURED PLYWOOD
ROOF				
R1	RAFTERS	7	1½ × 5½ × 99⅞"	DIMENSIONAL LUMBER (2x6)
R2	SHEATHING	2	¾ × 48 × 83½"	CDX PLYWOOD
R3	SHEATHING	2	¾ × 19½ × 48"	CDX PLYWOOD
R4	SHEATHING	1	¾ × 7 × 83½"	CDX PLYWOOD
R5	SHEATHING	1	¾ × 7 × 19½"	CDX PLYWOOD
TRIM				
T1	SKIRT BOARD - SIDE	2	¾ × 5½ × 66½"	DIMENSIONAL LUMBER (1x6)
T2	SKIRT BOARD - FRONT & BACK	2	¾ × 5½ × 92"	DIMENSIONAL LUMBER (1x6)
T3	CORNER BOARD - SIDE/BACK	2	¾ × 3½ × 78"	DIMENSIONAL LUMBER (1x4)
T4	CORNER BOARD - SIDE/FRONT	2	¾ × 3½ × 10¼"	DIMENSIONAL LUMBER (1x4)
T5	CORNER BOARD - BACK	2	¾ × 3½ × 76½"	DIMENSIONAL LUMBER (1x4)
T6	CORNER BOARD - FRONT	2	¾ × 3½ × 10½"	DIMENSIONAL LUMBER (1x4)
T7	DOOR CASING - STILE	2	¾ × 3½ × 80"	DIMENSIONAL LUMBER (1x4)
T8	DOOR CASING - RAIL	1	¾ × 3½ × 39½"	DIMENSIONAL LUMBER (1x4)
T9	SIDE BATTEN	2	¾ × 1½ × 83¾"	DIMENSIONAL LUMBER (1x2)
T10	FRONT BATTEN	1	¾ × 1½ × 12½"	DIMENSIONAL LUMBER (1x2)
T11	FASCIA BOARD - SIDE	2	¾ × 5½ × 101¾"	DIMENSIONAL LUMBER (1x6)
T12	FASCIA BOARD - FRONT/BACK	2	¾ × 6¹/₁₆ × 99"	DIMENSIONAL LUMBER (1x8)
HARDWARE REQUIRED				
	VENT COVERS	2	8 × 16"	
	PREHUNG DOOR	1	1⅜ × 32 × 80"	EXTERIOR
	BUILDING PAPER	100 sq. ft.		
	ROOFING MATERIAL		100 sq. ft.	YOUR CHOICE
	NAILS			
	SCREWS		#8 × 1½"	

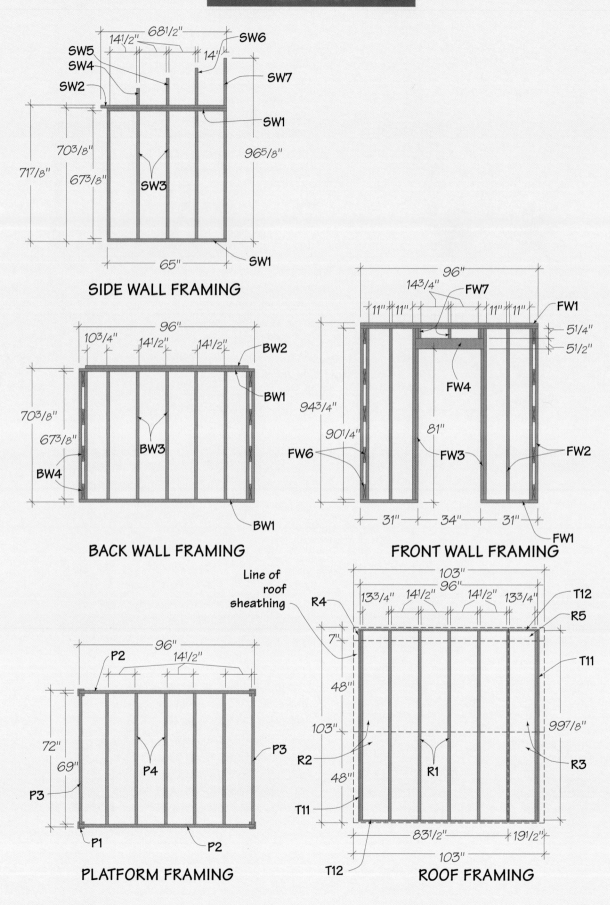

SIDE WALL FRAMING

BACK WALL FRAMING

FRONT WALL FRAMING

PLATFORM FRAMING

ROOF FRAMING

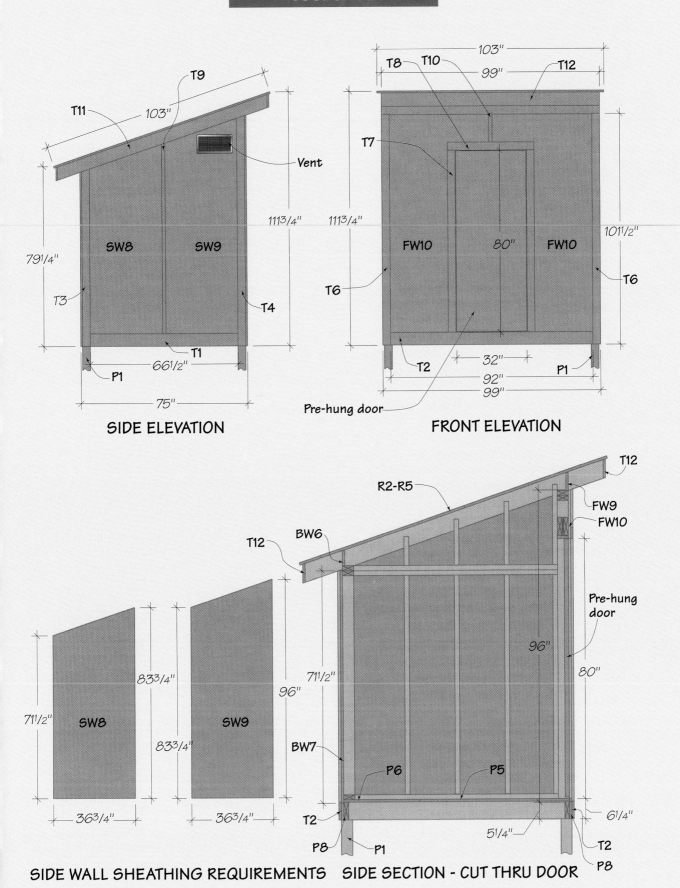

T9

T11

103"

Vent

79 1/4"

T3

SW8

SW9

T4

1113/4"

T1

P1

66 1/2"

75"

SIDE ELEVATION

T8

T10

103"

99"

T12

T7

1113/4"

FW10

80"

FW10

101 1/2"

T6

T6

T2

32"

P1

92"

99"

Pre-hung door

FRONT ELEVATION

T12

R2-R5

FW9

FW10

BW6

T12

Pre-hung door

96"

80"

83 3/4"

96"

71 1/2"

SW8

SW9

71 1/2"

BW7

83 3/4"

P6

P5

36 3/4"

36 3/4"

T2

5 1/4"

6 1/4"

P8

P1

T2

P8

SIDE WALL SHEATHING REQUIREMENTS   **SIDE SECTION - CUT THRU DOOR**

Shed kits like the one shown on pages 124 to 144 can be great time and money savers that are virtually foolproof to assemble. But the sizes and styles are somewhat limited, causing them to be easily identifiable as kit-built yard structures. For maximum versatility and to avoid the sameness of kit sheds, design and build your shed from scratch. Among yard structures, they are relatively simple to plan and to build in most cases.

The "stick-built" shed plan shown here is for a small, simple shed. It can be modified easily to reflect your particular size and style needs. It does not require an elaborate foundation—indeed, in some parts of the country it may be practical to simply set out four concrete blocks and construct the shed on top of them (as always, check with your local building department to determine structural requirements in your area).

Build the undercarriage

To create the undercarriage (post-and-joist structure) for a small structure such as a shed, you have several options. The traditional method is to use strings and batter boards to lay out the post hole locations, dig the holes, set the posts in concrete, then trim the tops off so they are level and at the correct height (See pages 27 to 29). But because the framework for the undercarriage in this case is relatively small and light (especially if you choose to use 2 × 4s instead of 2 × 6s), you can use a slightly less conventional method that is virtually foolproof: build the post-and-joist framework first, making sure it is square, use it as a guide for digging post holes, then set the assembly into the post holes. Before you begin, grade the shed site so it is level and well packed.

Construct the joist frame assembly from pressure-treated lumber (we used 2 × 6, but for smaller sheds you can usually get by with 2 × 4). Cut the joists to length, then join them using 16d common nails (galvanized) driven through the rim joists and into the ends of the interior joist members (nails have much greater sheer strength than deck screws). Or, you may use joist hangers with joist hanger nails instead. Check to make sure the assembly is square by measuring the diagonals.

Cut the posts to length (we used 4 × 4 treated lumber). To determine post length, add 2 inches to the depth of the post holes you plan to dig, allowing for a 4-in.-deep layer of rocks and gravel at the bottom of each hole. The posts normally should be long enough to extend beyond the frost line, but you may be able to get around this restriction in some cases.

Attach the posts to the joist frame. The frame should be positioned on the posts to create ledges on the outer edges the same thickness as your wall sheathing (½ to ¾ in. in most cases). Toe-nail through the frame and into the post on all sides, using galvanized nails *(See Detail 1).*

DETAIL 1: **Build the joist frame first, then toe-nail it to the posts. You'll know the resulting assembly is square and you can use it to lay out the post hole locations.**

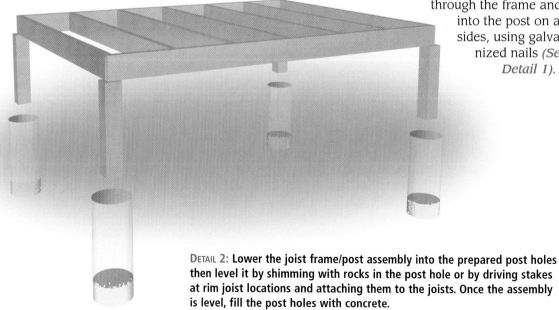

DETAIL 2: **Lower the joist frame/post assembly into the prepared post holes then level it by shimming with rocks in the post hole or by driving stakes at rim joist locations and attaching them to the joists. Once the assembly is level, fill the post holes with concrete.**

With a helper, set the undercarriage assembly (posts and joists) on the building site in the planned orientation and mark the post locations onto the ground. Remove the assembly and excavate the post holes—the diameter of each hole should be two to three times the post thickness. Use a story pole to gauge the hole depths. Add a 4-in.-thick layer of rock and gravel into each hole and tamp with a 2 × 4.

Again with a helper, lift the undercarriage assembly and set it in place with the posts in the post holes *(See Detail 2)*. Check with a level and adjust the position of the assembly by adding or removing subbase material from the holes or by lifting the assembly at low sides and securing it with stakes (attach the stakes with deck screws so they can be removed easily).

With the assembly secured in a level position, mix concrete (See pages 14 to 15) and shovel it into each post hole. Use a 2 × 4 to work the concrete down into the hole. Crown the concrete slightly with a

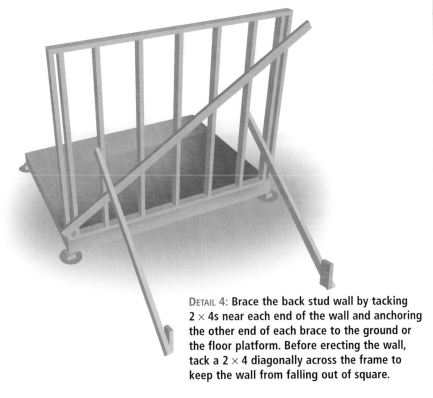

DETAIL 3: **Gang the cap and sole plates for the top and bottom together then lay out common stud locations using a framing square as a guide.**

trowel to shed water. Let the concrete cure overnight.

Cut floor sheathing to fit, making sure seams fall midway over the floor joists. Leave a gap of ⅛ in. or so between sheathing panels. We used ¾ in. exterior plywood for the floor. The edges of the floor should align with the outside edges of the joist frame. Apply construction adhesive to the tops of the joists before attaching the sheathing with 1½-in. deck screws.

Frame the walls & roof

You'll find it easier to build and square up each of the four stud wall frames, then attach them to the floor platform.

Build the front and back wall frames. Begin by cutting the sole and cap plates to length, then clamping them together edge-to-edge with ends aligned. Gang-mark the stud positions on the sole and top plates *(See Detail 3)*, using the layout diagrams on page 148 as a guide. Use a framing square to outline the stud locations. Designate one of the sole plates as the front and lay out the door jamb locations. NOTE: *The front wall layout shown on page 148 includes nailers near each corner of the shed for installing the interior wall coverings. If you do not plan to install interior wall coverings, you can eliminate these studs.*

Cut the full-height wall studs to length and nail the plates to the ends of the studs with 12d common nails. Cut the jack studs for the door opening to length, then fashion a header from 2× stock and ½ in. plywood (See *Tip*, next page). Nail the jack studs and header in position, then fill in above the header with shorter cripple studs. Once the entire wall frame is done, measure the diagonals to ensure that the walls are square. Tack a temporary diagonal brace across it to hold it in alignment while you position it on the floor platform.

Erect the walls. Move the newly framed walls onto the floor platform, beginning with the back wall. Have a couple of long 2 × 4 studs handy to brace the wall. With a helper, raise the wall into posi-

DETAIL 4: **Brace the back stud wall by tacking 2 × 4s near each end of the wall and anchoring the other end of each brace to the ground or the floor platform. Before erecting the wall, tack a 2 × 4 diagonally across the frame to keep the wall from falling out of square.**

tion. Align it flush with the edges of the floor platform. With a 4-foot level, bring the wall into rough plumb. Attach (temporarily) one end of a 2 × 4 brace to a wall stud, and nail the other end to a short 2 × 4 stake driven into the ground or cleat nailed to the floor. Add a brace near each end of the wall *(See Detail 4)*.

Double-check to make sure the back wall frame is level and plumb, then nail or screw the wall to the floor platform.

DETAIL 5: The doubled cap plates are interlocked at the back wall to stiffen the frame structure.

Fasten through the sole plate into the header joist in each stud bay.

Before installing the front wall, build and erect the side wall frames. Build the frames one at a time. Lay out the stud positions on the sole and top plates, and crosscut the necessary studs to length. Lay out the parts on a flat surface, nail them together and square the frame.

Move the first of the frames to the shed and lay it on the floor platform. Raise the frame into place and check the wall for plumb with a 4-foot level. When the wall is lined up properly, attach it to the back wall with 3 in. deck screws (nailing may throw the back wall out of position), then attach it to the floor platform. Attach the other side wall, then remove the braces

from the back wall.

Double the top plates *(See Detail 5)*. This ties the separate wall frames together. Measure from the front of the sidewall to the back of the back wall. Cut a 2 × 4 to that length. Lay it atop the top plate and screw it in place. Do the same at the other side. Then measure and cut a doubler for the back wall. This 2 × 4 will be shorter than the wall's top plate, since it must fit between the doublers already nailed to the sidewalls, which overlap the back wall top plate.

Erect the front wall frame. Plumb it up and screw it to the adjoining walls and to the floor platform. Finally, use a hand saw to cut the sole plate out of the rough opening for the door *(See Detail 6)*.

Install the rafters

This tool shed is capped, quite appropriately, by a *shed roof*. It features seven rafters nailed to the top plates. The eave end of each rafter is cut with a birdsmouth: a triangular cutout that allows the sloping rafter to rest solidly on the horizontal top plate. The ends of the rafters are trimmed with plumb cuts so they will form a line perpendicular to the ground when installed at a slope. This shed is made with 2 × 6 rafters, but for smaller sheds built in areas with minimal snow load,

DOOR HEADERS

½ in. plywood

Dimension lumber

Door headers are made by sandwiching a piece of ½ in. plywood between two lengths of dimensional lumber (2 × 6 is shown, but many sheds may require only 2 × 4). Join the elements with construction adhesive and 3 in. deck screws driven through both outer faces.

2 × 4s might be allowed, as long as the slope of the roof does not require you to cut the birdsmouth more than halfway into the rafter. Use 10-ft.-long pieces of dimension lumber to make the rafters.

To begin making a rafter, *plumb cut* one end. The pitch of the roof is 4-in-12, meaning the roof rises 4 in. for each foot of run. Use a framing square to mark cutting lines for the plumb cuts *(See Detail 7)*. Begin by aligning the 4-in. mark on the square's tongue and the 12-in. mark on the blade with the edge of the rafter, near one end. Draw a line along the tongue. This is the line for the plumb cut. Make the

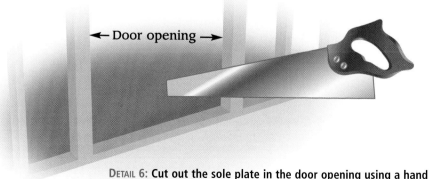

← Door opening →

DETAIL 6: Cut out the sole plate in the door opening using a hand saw or a reciprocating saw with the blade installed backwards.

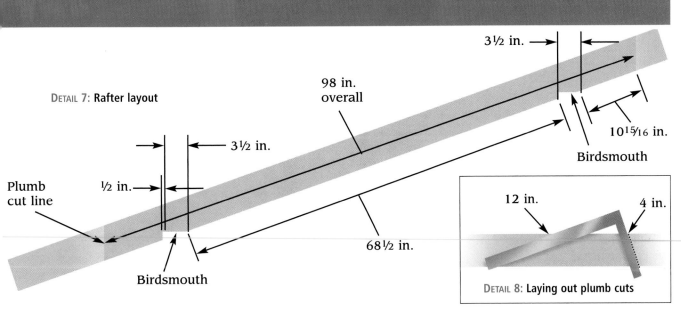

DETAIL 7: **Rafter layout**

3½ in.

98 in. overall

3½ in.

10¹⁵⁄₁₆ in.

Birdsmouth

Plumb cut line

½ in.

12 in.

4 in.

68½ in.

Birdsmouth

DETAIL 8: **Laying out plumb cuts**

plumb cut using a circular saw and straightedge cutting guide. Measure 98 in. along the top edge of the rafter and at that point lay out a second plumb cut, parallel to the first. Make the second cut to trim the rafter to length.

(See Detail 8) Now, measure 10¹⁵⁄₁₆ in. from each plumb cut along the bottom edge of the rafter and scribe *building lines* parallel to the plumb cuts to mark the outer surface of the shed's framing. To lay out the first birdsmouth, set the outside corner of your framing square dead on the edge of the rafter at the building line. Align the blade on that line. Scribe a 3½ in. line along the tongue of the square. This marks the seat cut. Shift the square around and mark another line parallel to the plumb cut (this is the *inside building line*), which establishes the back of the birdsmouth. Cut the birdsmouth with a jig saw.

Measure along the bottom edge of the rafter and lay out the second birdsmouth in much the same way. Note on the layout that the back birdsmouth has a 4-in. seat cut (compared to 3½ in. on the front), to accommodate the sheathing. Cut this birdsmouth. Lay out and cut all the rafters.

Install the outer rafters. With a helper, position them so the seat

cuts rest flush on the cap plates (the ½ in. gap should be at the outside edge of the rear cap plate). The outer faces of the rafters should be aligned with the outside edges of the wall frame. Attach the rafters by toenailing them to the cap plates with 16d common nails (See Detail 9).

Attach the interior rafters according to the spacing layout shown on page 148.

Cut and install cripple studs between the top plates on the side walls and the outer rafters. NOTE: *The traditional way to build shed side walls is to cut full-height studs that span all the way from the sole plate to the rafters and are cut at the top to follow the rafter line. We designed the shed shown here using "platform" type construction because it is easier to square up and is generally less vulnerable to errors in construction.* The best way to produce the cripples is to take a rough measurement from plate to rafter above each regular stud in the side wall. Add about 10 in. to each measurement and cut pieces of

2 × 4 to that length. One by one, set the cripples in place, level them and scribe the edges of each cripple along the bottom edge of the rafter, marking the shoulder of the lap. Also scribe each cripple along the top edge of the rafter to mark it for cutting to length. Cut the cripples to length, then lay out 1¾-in.-deep lap cuts on each cripple, extending between the rafter lines. Trim each cripple to length by cutting along the top rafter line. Make the *shoulder* portion on each lap cut with your circular saw set to 1¾ in. cut-

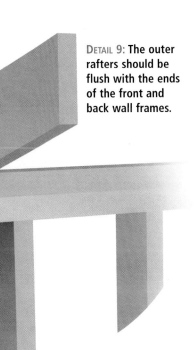

DETAIL 9: **The outer rafters should be flush with the ends of the front and back wall frames.**

ting depth. Use a reciprocating saw or hand saw to make the *cheek cuts.*

Install the cripples by toe-nailing them to the cap plate and face-nailing them through the lap joint and into the rafter *(See Detail 10).*

Install the wall & roof coverings

When selecting materials for sheathing and siding your shed, consider several factors: the type of siding used on nearby structures and your house; the amount of exposure the shed will receive; the difficulty of installing the siding; and whether or not you intend to install interior wall coverings. The fastest (and usually cheapest) product for cladding shed walls is plywood siding. It is sold in 4 × 8 sheets with either a smooth or rough-textured surface. For a shed, ⅜-in.-thick stock generally is adequate, but we suggest ⅝ in. siding for added stability and durability.

Cut and install the roof sheathing. We used ¾-in. exterior plywood sheathing. Make sure the seams fall along rafters. The edges of the sheathing panels should overhang the rafter frame by 3 in. on all sides. Use 1½-in. deck screws or ring shank nails to attach the sheathing. The seams and edges of the siding will be trimmed later.

Trim out the roof frame *(See Detail 11)* by cutting and attaching 1 × 6 furring boards to the outside faces of the outer rafters (the ends should be cut at the same plumb cut angle as the rafters). Then, cut and attach fascia boards to the front and back so the ends cover the edges of the furring strips. To make these parts, the best method is to bevel-rip 1 × 8 stock at the slope angle (4-in-12). This way, the bottom and top of each fascia board will continue the line of the roof. Nail the fascia to the ends of the rafters.

Cut and attach side panels to the wall frames, according to the sheathing pattern shown on page 149 (but double-check your measurements first for dimension and to make sure the seam between panels will fall over the middle of a stud). Use galvanized siding nails driven at 8 in. intervals along each stud and along the cap plate and sole plate. Don't butt the sheets of plywood tightly together; leave a gap of about ⅟16 in. at seams.

Attach the front siding panels. The framework for the shed is sized so you should be able to cover the wall with two full-length sheets of siding that are flush with the top of the doubled cap plate and the top edge of the rim joist. The siding should cover the door opening.

Before installing siding on the back wall, cut out the door opening in the front wall sheathing. Drive a nail at each corner of the opening,

Cripple stud

⅝-in. gap for siding

Cheek

Shoulder

1¾ in.

Cripple stud detail

DETAIL 10: Cripple studs are installed in the side wall frames between the cap plates and the tops of the rafters. A 1¾-in.-deep lap is cut in the top of each cripple to provide a support surface for the rafter. The cripple is nailed or screwed to the rafter, through the lap joint.

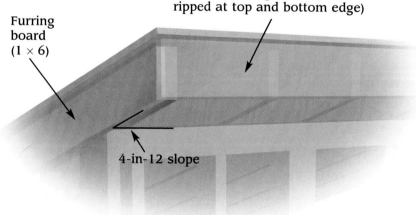

Fascia, shown ghosted (1 × 8, bevel-ripped at top and bottom edge)

Furring board (1 × 6)

4-in-12 slope

DETAIL 11: Cut two 1 × 6 furring boards with the same plumb cut angles as the rafters and tack one board to the outside face of each rafter. Then, bevel-rip 1 × 8s along the top and bottom edge to produce fascia boards that follow the roof slope and completely cover the ends of the rafters.

then connect the nail heads with chalklines to outline the door opening *(See Detail 12)*. Cut the opening with a circular saw, using a straightedge if you need to. Stop the cuts short of the corners and finish them with a hand saw or reciprocating saw. Clean up the cut edges with a handsaw so the cutout is smooth and even with the 2 × 4s that frame the opening.

Cut and install siding for the back wall, slipping the top edge of each piece into the gaps at the backs of the rafter birdsmouths.

Install the roof covering. Begin by tacking metal or vinyl drip edge to the back (low) edge and sides of the roof. If you are installing regular tab-style shingles, you'll need to staple strips of building paper to the sheathing, laid with 6-in. overlaps beginning at the low end of the roof. After the last piece of building paper is installed, tack drip edge along the high edge of the roof, overlapping the drip edge, then install the shingles (See pages 43 to 45 for more information on shingling). If you're using roll roofing to cover the shed, no underlayment is required. See *Roll Roofing*, page 156, for instructions.

Install *bird blocking* cut from scrap siding or 1 × 6 pieces in the gap between the double cap plates and the underside of the roof sheathing at the front and back of the shed *(See Detail 13)*. Measure and cut each piece to fit. Tack nailing strips around each opening so the blocking pieces will be flush with the siding.

TIP: To minimize mess and avoid masking, apply paint or wood protectant to the siding before installing the trim. Also prime and paint the trim pieces after cutting them to size, but before installation.

DETAIL 12: **Install sheathing over the door framing, then cut out around the framed opening to create the opening for the door. To mark the opening on the sheathing, drive a nail through the sheathing at each corner of the framed opening, then connect the nail points with chalklines.**

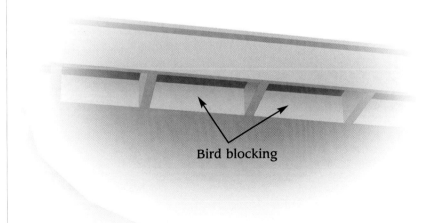

Bird blocking

DETAIL 13: **Cut pieces of 1 × 6 or siding material (called *bird blocking*) and fit them into the gaps between the tops of the front and back walls and the underside of the sheathing.**

Hang the door & install siding trim

The shed design is sized to accept a standard 32-in.-wide by 80-in.-high prehung exterior door. The door opening should be 34 in. wide and 81 in. high to allow for the door jambs and shims.

Hang the door in the door opening, according to the manufacturer's installation instructions.

Before installing the 1 × 4 casing, cut strips of scrap siding to fur out the rim joists, then attach 1 × 6 skirt boards to cover the rim joist areas. Install the side skirting first, flush with the furred-out faces of the front and back rim joists. Then cut the front and back skirt boards long enough to cover the ends of the side skirts. Attach the skirt boards with 6d galvanized finish nails.

Cut and attach 1 × 4 door casing pieces *(See Detail 14)*. Cut the side casing strips to fit between the skirt board and the bottom of the door head jamb. The ends of the top casing should be flush with the outside edges of the side casing.

Cut and install 1 × 4 corner boards, beginning at the sides

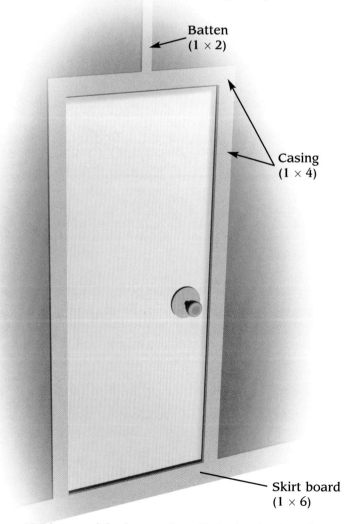

Batten
(1 × 2)

Casing
(1 × 4)

Skirt board
(1 × 6)

DETAIL 14: **Trim around the door opening with 1 × 4 casing, butted at the header joints, and a 1 × 6 skirt board to cover the rim joist. 1 × 2 battens are attached to conceal vertical seams.**

ROLL ROOFING

Roll roofing is a fiberglass-based roof covering product made in 36-in.-wide strips that are designed for either *single coverage* or *double coverage* installation—in most cases, single coverage rolls will be adequate for a shed. It can be installed directly to the roof sheathing in most areas, requiring no building-paper underlayment. It is designed for flat roofs or roofs with a pitch of 4-in-12 or less. Because it doesn't require underlayment and can be rolled out in long strips, it is generally faster to install than other roofing products.

To install single coverage roll roofing, begin by cutting 12-in.-wide starter strips of roofing and attaching them around the perimeter of the roof. Attach the starter strip at the low end first by bonding it to the sheathing with fibrous roof cement, then driving roofing nails at 4 in. intervals around all edges. The starter strip should stop about ¼ in. before reaching the edges of the drip edge. Cut and attach starter strips along both sides (the rake edges) in the same fashion as the front edge starter strip. Then attach a starter strip at the high edge of the roof.

After the starter strips are all in place, begin to install the full-width strips. Starting at the low end of the roof, cover the starter strips with roof cement. Lay the first strip so it is flush with the edges of the front and side starter strips and seat it in the roof cement. Drive roofing nails along the top edge of the strip according to the nail-spacing requirement recommended by the roofing manufacturer. After the first strip is installed, apply a 3-in.-wide layer of roof cement along the top edge and to the side starter strips in the coverage area. Roll out the second strip so it overlaps the first strip by 3 inches, concealing the nail heads and resulting in a 33-in. reveal. Nail the second strip in place, and work your way up toward the top of the roof. Trim the last strip as needed to neatly cover the top starter strip, fully bonding it with roof cement as you did at the low end and sides. Apply a dab of roof cement over all the exposed nailheads at the top edge, then tack drip edge molding over the roofing at the top edge.

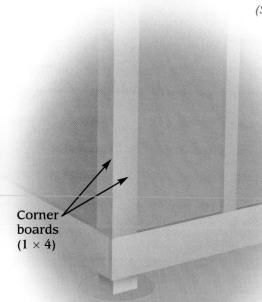

Corner
boards
(1 × 4)

DETAIL 15: **Finish trimming out the siding by installing 1 × 4 corner boards. The boards on the front and back walls should overlap the edges of the side corner boards.**

(See Detail 15). The side corner boards should extend from the bottom of the the skirt board to the underside of the roof sheathing. Cut the top edge at an angle to match the slope of the roof so it will fit tightly against the sheathing. The front and back corner boards should cover the edges of the side corner boards and also should be trimmed (beveled) at the top to match the roof slope.

Cut and install strips of 1 × 2 to make battens for covering the vertical seams between siding panels.

Finishing touches

To create ventilation in the shed, cut a hole near the top of each side wall, over a stud cavity. Cover the openings with louvered soffit vent covers after you paint the shed *(See Detail 16).*

Finish the interior (optional). The doubled corner posts shown here provide nailing surfaces for installing interior wall coverings. Many sheds, however, do not need interior walls. If you choose to install them, ⅜-in.-thick oriented strand board (OSB) is a good material choice.

To prolong its life, paint the floor with enamel floor paint.

Caulk around all the exterior trim pieces and between the roof sheathing and the walls.

DETAIL 16: **Cut openings at the top of each side wall to create air flow for ventilation. Cover the vent holes with louvered soffit vent covers (shown below) or insect screening.**

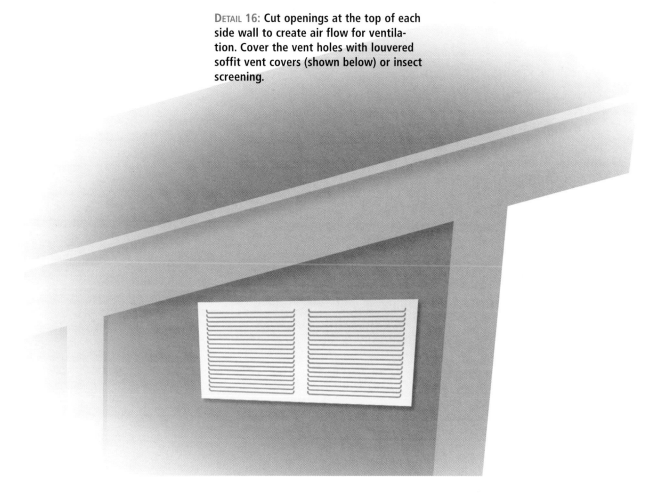

Index

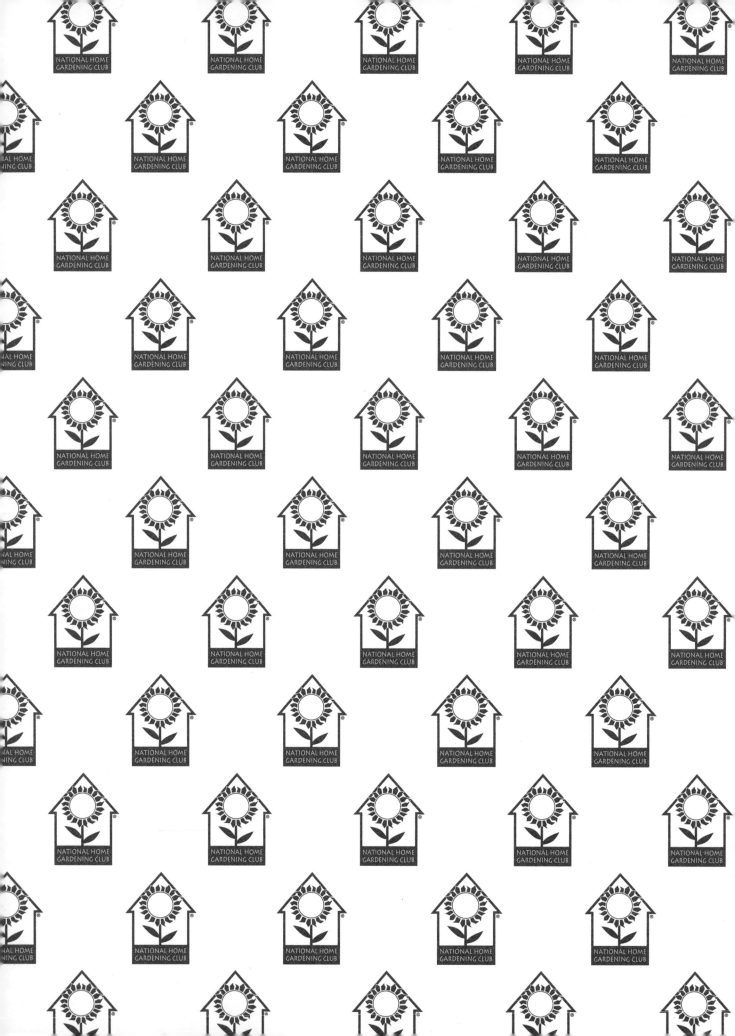